AN
EXTRAORDINARY
SILENCE

AN EXTRAORDINARY
____SILENCE____

The Emergence of a
Deeply Disturbed Child

David C. Cipolloni

BERGIN & GARVEY
Westport, Connecticut • London

Library of Congress Cataloging-in-Publication Data

Cipolloni, David C.
  An extraordinary silence : the emergence of a deeply disturbed
child / David C. Cipolloni.
     p.   cm.
  ISBN 0-89789-357-3 (acid-free paper)
    1. Autistic children—Rehabilitation—Case studies. 2. Child
psychotherapy—Case studies. 3. Psychotherapist and patient—Case
studies. I. Title.
  RJ506.A9C5 1993
  618.92'8982—dc20   93-15184

British Library Cataloguing in Publication Data is available.

Library of Congress Catalog Card Number: 93-15184
ISBN: 0-89789-357-3

First published in 1993

Bergin & Garvey, 88 Post Road West, Westport, CT 06881
An imprint of Greenwood Publishing Group, Inc.

Printed in the United States of America

The paper used in this book complies with the
Permanent Paper Standard issued by the National
Information Standards Organization (Z39.48-1984).

10 9 8 7 6 5 4 3 2 1

To Bob S.
for believing.

Contents

Preface

This is a work of non-fiction.

In order to respect the confidential nature of the subject matter and to protect the privacy of the principal characters, their names have been changed, and any identifying locations, circumstances, and events have been altered.

I have written this with great respect for all the children and families that are presented or referred to here, and for all of the others that I have worked with that are in many ways represented here.

I do not presume, intend, nor wish to rebuke, blame, or judge any of the actual people involved. I do hope to help unravel the gnarled and confusing issues of responsibility and action in dealing with children of difficulty and uniqueness, perhaps to cast another angle of light upon the purposes and effects of categorizing, theorizing about, and perceiving them.

I came to know a deep empathy with each of the children and family members and it is from that knowing, of the sheer and utter pain and helplessness and anger and loneliness of their experience, that I came to write this.

David Cipolloni
November 1992
Flagler Beach, Florida

AN EXTRAORDINARY SILENCE

1

In the Box

His choice was not between playacting and action. His choice was between playacting and no action at all. There are situations in which people are condemned to playact.

Milan Kundera

We are inside the large cardboard refrigerator box. It echoes softly with puffs of breath, the thin scurrying of grains of dirt, the rhythmic tapping of the backs of his fingers.

I had been following Sean around all morning, wanting to be with him. I would sit next to him and watch how he would spit a tiny puddle of saliva on the linoleum and, with a certain grace, hold his hand palm upward, slender fingers rolling lightly upon the shiny, moist pool.

He would carry on, indifferent to me, even seemingly oblivious, but I detected his annoyance. He would abruptly rise and wander to another spot, squatting unobtrusively in a corner, behind some furniture, beneath the wall heater. I followed and watched as he resumed spitting and flapping, as he found pockets of dust or sand and with a measured breath blew delicately, focusing on the particles' movements.

I wanted to be with him and he continued to move away, so we are now inside the box where Sean can no longer avoid my presence.

This boy.

This strange, lovely, enigmatic, stolid boy, I realize, is already affecting me deeply. He is crouched on all fours, his face inches from the floor, wholly absorbed in the forming of swirling patterns. So unreachable. After a month of my constant trying, still so unreachable, so unknown, so frustrating.

I begin to speak. I have no reason to think he is listening to me. Yet I believe he hears me, that he understands what I am saying, although I don't really know why.

I tell him that he is trapped, that he won't be tolerated much longer, that he'll be sent away. I say that I believe there is more to him than he has been showing me, much more, and that he is hiding. Hiding and angry and very hurt, and very proud. Afraid, yet, also, strong. And that he is indeed trapped.

I speak to him. I focus acutely on the singularity of this child. I look to the essence of who he is, of what is happening in his life.

Here we are, inside a cardboard box, dark, still. Underneath his shields, his defenses, his weird dances that are so convincing, so captivating, I sense another part of him. I want to connect with him there, to acknowledge that part of him as worthy, valid. It is there, I realize, that I find him beautiful and special.

I speak to Sean, reaching to him with my entire being, speaking this with words only as a way to shuttle my intuited vision from soul to soul. I feel the box fill with the intensity of my desire to reach him, to touch this hidden private self of his that I perceive.

The box fills with the intensity of my intent, emanating, soliciting, and, as I speak, Sean begins loudly vocalizing to drown out my voice, burying his face in his arms so that I may not be there. I fully address this troubled small person with my unwavering intent and then he turns to me, eyes swollen with tears, looking directly at me while putting his hand over my mouth. The box fills with something alive, tingling, sobering. I embrace Sean as he cries piteously, a cry of the profoundly alone.

2

Sean Observed

He sat then as children do, immured in his particular lonely world then, having built a magnetic wall of detachment.

Anais Nin

I first meet Sean and his mother waiting for me in the office. She is a handsome woman, well dressed, and although we are close in age, she carries herself as if burdened with greater years. She is intelligent and articulate, and her eyes remain clear and direct with my own. While I talk with her, Sean makes little gooing and cooing noises, smiling sort of idiotically, squeezing his eyes tightly between stealing quick glances at me. He bubbles saliva from his mouth onto the lining of his jacket, which is wet and matted, pressing it with his tongue.

He is about as tall as you would expect a nine-year-old to be but lanky, slender, though quite strong, quick, and agile. A good-looking boy with fine, blond-brown hair, clear fawnlike hazel eyes, smooth complexion over high cheekbones and angular features. He is very well coordinated, with superb balance and fast reflexes.

Even when he seems fully absorbed in blowing dust or patting a pool of spittle, I suspect he is still aware of everything, everything going on around him.

Like a cat.

Sean does not speak at all. Just makes tiny sounds to himself. I think he hears quite well but he acts as though he doesn't comprehend the simplest request without guidance or cues. At other times he suddenly understands something I ask, even something fairly complex.

He does not look people in their eyes, almost like they are not there. He only looks at me for the briefest instant. He seems so indifferent, so aloof, almost supercilious.

He looks frail, fragile for a nine-year-old. It's pathetic to watch him always blowing or tapping, spitting or pressing his tongue on things. He is stealthful at hiding, taking a piece of cellophane or something furry, careful, fearful. Left alone, it seems to give him such solace.

Sean lets me play with him, tickling, roughing him up, but like an infant and nothing like a little boy. He waits for me to act on him, doesn't reach out. He purses his lips, rolling his tongue out between them. Rubs his eyes with his fists, gooing and cooing, particularly when I look too directly or steadily at him. I can't move too fast. I must first tell him what I am about to do—"Oh, let's see those ears!" I can't cover his head, can't pick him up or roll him off the ground with my body. I do these things, any kind of wrong thing, and he becomes petrified, whining, scrambling to get away. It is so touch and go.

Sean seems to avoid his father. With his mother he is docile, passive, infantile. Being unsure how to regard their son, to Jeff and Joan he is their Sean-Sean, their overgrown baby. It is virtually the only way he will relate with them. Sean-Sean, their relentless problem, peculiarity, embarrassment, disappointment that weighs heavily on them. They are not happy people. Their Sean-Sean does not bring them much joy.

I spend time with Sean, hour upon hour, day after day, and I begin to realize the full impact of how utterly unto himself he is. Sean does not approach people, does not look for their company or companionship. He shows no desire to play ball or sports or games or even hang out with other kids. Objects, toys mean virtually nothing to him. He has no interest in playing with cars and trucks, does not act out imaginary dramas with figures of people. He ignores building blocks and puzzles, crayons and finger paints, chalkboards and scissors. He never watches television. With anything unfamiliar Sean appears overwhelmed and tries to hide, under his jacket, beneath my arm, behind furniture, or if he can't, then he tightly closes his eyes. Sometimes he gets agitated and I have to figure out what worked him up. It might be just to use the toilet or get a drink of water, but often he stays upset, whining and crying, tragic, inconsolable.

Until he is interrupted or directed somehow, Sean will pass his entire waking day finding various things and places to blow, flap, spit, and press his tongue upon. This brings out his only motivation, with the same tenacity and single-mindedness as a plant's tropisms seek light and water. And I watch him, I catch a look in his eyes and something stirs there. It is a depth of understanding and ability, somewhere securely inside.

It all, all of it, seems so intentional, so eerily deliberate.

3

Beginning Encounters

A man considers himself dead, cold, inert; then the right flame
appears and he flies into it like a moth.

Martin Cruz Smith

I keep reading at the table when Sean comes into the room. I don't
give him my usual greeting that he never returns, don't even turn
to look at him. With his casual, debonair walk he goes to his
favorite area and kneels to collect wispy balls of dust with well-
practiced puffs of his breath. I can easily observe him in my
periphery without looking up and I continue to act engrossed in my
book. He, too, appears content to be left alone. After flapping and
blowing on the dust awhile, he curls up in the armchair with the
large stuffed lion in his lap and presses his mouth on the fur. He
salivates on it, blows a little, licks it with his tongue, lightly flaps
on the sogginess with the backs of his fingers, gooing and cooing.
Really enjoying himself. I stay at the table. Sean saunters to the
mirror, lies on the floor in front of it, salivates and presses his
tongue on its surface. Then on the floor. Then the carpet. Not
once does he look at me.

This goes on for over an hour. I watch as Sean spits and
flaps on his pant leg, on his sleeve. He pauses, sitting on the
carpet, and urinates copiously, thoroughly wetting his pants down
to his socks and shoes. I continue to sit. Sean still does not look
at me. He walks over to the open, screenless window, looks out,
then climbs onto the sill. It is over two floors to the ground below.

Sean finds some dust on the ledge, blowing and flapping, convincingly indifferent to the height. He leans out precariously, stands up, turns with his back to the empty space, searching the window frame for interesting cobwebs.

I have no reason to be assured of Sean's sense of balance or awareness of height. All it would take is one slip of his wet shoes. Yet somehow I feel sure of him, and I sit. Very nervously, I sit. Like a dancer, with unpredictable but well-controlled movements, Sean stays on the narrow sill perhaps fifteen minutes or so, and then climbs back into the room. I haven't realized I've been holding my breath. I haven't looked up and Sean hasn't looked over.

I know I'm not fooling him any more than he's not fooling me. Sean steps on the back of a chair and then, lithe as a cat, pulls himself up on top of the room divider. He stands and walks along this four-inch-wide wall, seven feet above the floor, staring upward toward the ceiling and vocalizing his little sounds. Amazing. He sits on the wall and takes off all his clothes, then resumes walking back and forth, making his noises. The wall sways. I continue the standoff.

The lunch bell sounds. I stay at the table. I know he must be hungry. Sean stays on the wall for another twenty minutes and then climbs down. He plays with his wet pants on the floor, spits on the linoleum and blows on it, flaps some dust. He comes over behind me in his inimitable walk, stark naked, looking up to the ceiling while making his soft, melodious sounds and stands with his back against mine. I wait. He turns to face my back and plays gently with my hair. I do not turn around.

"Hello Sean. I'm really glad you came over."

He stops playing with my hair. Silence.

"I'd really like to see you."

Silence.

Sean walks around the table and stands in front of me, grinning, naked and grinning, saying a hard consonant, "Gheeee!"

I believe it is from that point on I know I am dealing with a master. For weeks now I have been soliciting Sean. His compliance is like a willing but obtuse puppy. If I call him he comes. If I ask him to sit, he sits. Simple things. But anything more—"Hey, Sean, take the book over to the shelf"—he just stares at me with a puzzled look, doing only what I show him with gestures or cues. If I don't continually give him directives he invariably returns to one of his routines.

So I move into his space.

At first he regards my presence as an interruption, almost an insult to his private puffing and salivating and flapping, and he moves away. I persist, and I follow him until he settles somewhere. I usually do not speak to him. If I say anything I comment, sincerely, on the strangely fascinating qualities of what he finds so absorbing. The delicate movement of dust. The soft patterns he makes on fur with his breath. The smooth sheen he admires by wetting surfaces. The graceful rhythmic tapping with his fingers. Sometimes I imitate what he does, sometimes I simply watch. At times I even try to puff gently with him on his collection of dust or tap together on a stretched piece of cellophane; annoyed, he moves away.

> Play time.
> "Hey, Sean."
> He looks at me, breathy "Uhnnnh." Turns away.
> "Let's see what you brought today, okay?"
> Slight grin. He knows what's coming.
> I sit on the carpet in front of the large mirror and reach for his arm. Pale, thin. "Hey, look at this arm. Pretty nice. All that muscle inside, all the way up here." I'm grabbing and kneading and squeezing. "Look at this, bends right here, back and forth." I move his joints, stretching and folding, flopping his limp hand and forearm around like a ragdoll.
> "What's this? What's under here?"
> He squeals in delight, pulls away as I poke his armpit. I follow with his turn, keeping contact.
> "Nice shirt. Look at this. Blue stripes, some white here."
> He reflexively imitates my pointing, abruptly touches his shirt and looks away.
> I lift it from his pants. Quickly.
> "Wow! Look at this belly!" Blowing loud bubbles on it

with my mouth. Catch him off guard before he can stop me. Deep, abandoned laughter, sparkling eyes.

I indulge his infantilism. I play with him mercilessly, intrusively, always keeping contact, sensing him, reading his cues. He allows this. He laughs, grins, giggles, vocalizes goos and ghees and coos of contentment. He lets me do these things to him as if to please me and he has nothing to do with it. Because as soon as I pause, to gauge his reaction or wait for some initiation from him, he simply turns away and resumes puffing and flapping.

I tire of the continual, predictable rhythms. After playing energetically with his feet, pulling on his toes and biting his soles and heels, I take some lotion warmed between my palms and slowly, firmly massage his feet. Then his calves. He reaches to stop me and I take his arm, massage his hand, forearm, elbow. He is a bit unnerved at this sudden intimacy, tensing, but I stay with him, gentle and firm. We sit before the mirror and I recreate the same discovery process of his body I have already been doing in the rough and vigorous play. Stroking, caressing, celebrating the marvels of his fingers and toes and limbs, finding his heartbeat and pulses, examining the faint blue lines of veins and arteries trailing beneath pale translucent skin. Sean abandons to my touch, my voice. He watches, calm and absorbent, while I explore the features of his face, outlining nose and eyes and mouth, cheeks and ears and chin, teeth and lips and forehead. I explore his face without the mirror, remaining in a world of mutual silence, with Sean looking direct and tranquil into my eyes.

Quickly, it seems, I have come far with Sean, in learning something of him, in establishing a kind of equilibrium in our being together. It strikes me as extremely significant, as it is equally subtle and almost invisible in the flow from one day to the next, that I certainly would not have gotten anywhere if Sean was not receptive. He did not have to let me stay beside him and silently synchronize blowing on feathers and dust. He did not have to so eagerly allow me to toss him around and tickle him and rough him up. Nor to lie quietly and intimately with no pretense of games or play. He did not, I remind myself constantly, have to let me in. He has clearly kept so many out.

What seems fairly natural and casual in the course of a relationship with a child are the very things Sean has avoided and withheld virtually without exception for over nine years with his own mother, father, and brothers. Of this I am profoundly, acutely aware. I am both stunned and encouraged by the essence of what is happening, that Sean is, in fact, communicating. That he is not frozen within his rituals, not as oblivious and indifferent to the world as the world has concluded.

In his own way, Sean is communicating. And I want more. Which is why I did not greet him when he came into the room.

4

Disrupted Territory

Imagine darkness.
In the darkness that faces outward from the sun a mute spirit woke.

Ursula LeGuin

I want to learn more.

After many weeks, I arrange to visit Sean's parents at their home one evening, an older house that has required continual upkeep; a presentable, average, working-class house along a quiet side street shaded by canopies of live oaks.

Jeff greets me cordially with a muscular handshake. Inside, we seat ourselves around a blaring television, the furnishings worn and colorless. Joan calls to me cheerfully from the kitchen with an air of easy familiarity.

She comes out to join us. Each sits in a separate chair. The television still blares. I try to talk over the noise, but I then have to suggest that they turn it down. Effusive with apology, they scramble to the set. I don't believe they had even noticed. Jeff reduces the volume, barely detectable, but leaves the picture on.

I ask about their lives. About their marriage, their family, about Sean and the two other boys. Clearly these are disturbing questions, likely ones never posed to them. Eye contact is rough. The television draws their attention as their gazes anxiously search for something to settle on. Long, vacant pauses. Their voices trail off inaudibly. They abruptly snap into focus as I repeat a question, then fade away again, blankly staring at the television or into space. They do not relate to what I tell them about Sean. In turn, I can not make much sense of either Sean's history or any projection into his future. The image is fixed, like a curious insect in amber, as if neither Sean nor time will change.

I end my visit, leaving these parents as very confused, and very confusing. They certainly are quite disturbed in allowing my intrusion. I entered their home, their lives, my intimacies with their son, like sunlight in shadow. The dust flutters in the air, and they squint like blinking, helpless moles.

I want to mix it up, push him. I want to see more of what Sean has. It is a glorious day at the beach, sensually alive with the caressing wind, the soothing lull of rolling waves. The sun is a sheet of yellow heat under a richly blue sky.

Sean is ecstatic. "EEEEEEE!"

He leaps across the sand to the lapping shallows of water, glistening, inviting. He can't flap fast enough.

I tap with him a little. I drop handfuls of wet sugary sand, like pancake batter, onto his hands. He watches them disappear. Then he tries it himself. I drip sand on his leg. He watches. I cover both his legs with the wet sand, burying them completely. Sean finds this quite funny and giggles.

I take his hand, pull him up and go to the water.

"EEEEEEE!"

I splash water on him, rinsing the sand. I grab his hand and we run through the shallows. When I let go, he squats to blow and flap the surface. I take his hand again.

"Let's go in." The waves break on his waist, his chest. I lift him by his hands to jump the ones that are higher. As we wade deeper I hold him, he wraps his arms around my neck and his legs encircle my waist. Tightly. But he does not seem afraid, just tense, excited. Sean trusts me as we jump and bounce together with the crashing waves, jumping with that wonderful, easy buoyancy of the ocean. A few splash our faces, a few bury our heads. He sputters, blinks his eyes widely.

I spread out a lunch on the blanket but Sean is so overwhelmed he does not want to eat. I call to him to come from the tidepools where he is flapping. He sits on the blanket facing away from me, gazing off to the sea, absently blowing and flapping the sand lightly.

"Let's jog."

He runs, lithe and effortless, alongside. Quite bored. I pick up the pace and after about a mile slow down, continuing to walk.

"Look at that sky, Sean! What a beautiful day! See those clouds? Those are my favorite. Cumulonimbus. Big ol' things. See how they climb and climb, like a huge mountain?"

He glances up at my pointing finger.

"And those puffy ones are cumulus, like balls of fluffy cotton."

A cursory glance.

"Sean, look! An osprey! Watch him, watch. He's going to dive."

Sean looks, reveals nothing. We keep walking.

"Feel the wind." I hold my hand out, fingers spread, palm open as if pushing the breezes.

He imitates without emotion or expression.

"See the birds?"

He points automatically, holding his outstretched arm out after he looks away.

"Gulls. That's their name, seagulls."

We have walked a long way and Sean is becoming restless. It has been a while since he has had a chance to flap or blow. Must be getting to him.

"See that, Sean? It's a crab hole. Let's look for some more. Here's another one."

I've got him zigzagging along the tideline, stopping and pointing at holes with me, his face a blank.

"Show me one."

Unbelievable. On his own, he points one out.

"All right!" I tousle his head.

It occurs to me that the more Sean spends his time compulsively with his routines the less he can interact with the world. And the more that he will be acted upon, directed. Or left alone.

On the playground Sean flaps interminably on the sand or

blows on dried leaves or spits on the sliding board. I interrupt him, directing him to swing, to climb the bars, to slide, to jog. He does these things with me or as I tell him but seems thoroughly and consummately bored. Flapping and spitting and such are infinitely more interesting, and he invariably finds a way to do them as water finds its way downhill. With crafty, inventive obstinacy, he will do them. Sauntering along, he heads for a swing-set only to slink behind a tree where I find him feverishly blowing and flapping the dirt.

We take walks. We go through sordid, run-down neighborhoods and suburbs swept with lavish homes, beside railroad tracks and next to waterways. We walk along a main highway for over two miles to a small business district of hardware stores, toy departments, a library, cafes, a park near a river. It is long and hot and demanding. I speak with Sean always about the entire experience, what we see and smell, the noises, the weather. We sit on a bus bench at a busy corner, watching.

We spend hours in a shopping mall with its relentless overstimulation. At the airport, watching people arrive and depart, at baggage moving along the conveyer, looking through the fence at the massive jets landing and taxiing and, as if defiantly, rising into the air. We ride elevators and public buses, eat in restaurants and fast food outlets, buy stamps in a post office.

I take Sean to places and expose him to things I know are entirely new to him. While he is flooded with the variety and stimulation, I am acutely intent upon keeping him engaged and focused. I talk descriptions, directions, running monologues, and almost always I am somehow physically touching him. Resting my hand on his shoulder, carrying him on my back, stopping to play a little or to sit and have some sort of exchange. Somehow, always checking in.

And Sean absorbs it all in calm alertness, smoothly accommodating to everything with his air of indifference.

We drive to the inlet in my car. A long rock jetty thrusts into the ocean, with waves crashing and foaming and battering against it. Sailboats and squatty, powerful commercial fishers and loud, sleek racers and elegant windsurfers move in and out the channel. Wide, shallow sandbars sweep into the bay with islands of mangroves, alive with gulls and terns and egrets and herons. I show Sean the lighthouse, that peculiar structure like a candy-striped pencil.

All this, and no reaction.

Nothing. Or so it appears.

I know Sean is doing more than tolerating, more than witnessing, more than absorbing. He is not as passive as he affects. He is processing it. All of it, everything.

Somehow, I know this.

5

Responding to Presence

What's the point of being alive, she said, it you're not going to communicate?

Kurt Vonnegut, Jr.

We lie in the grass under tall, rustling maple trees while crisp leaves float down above our heads, and I talk a world of clouds and sky and birds, of smells and sounds and textures, of the brush of the wind and the play of sunlight and while all this is sincere and truthful, what I am really talking to this elusive boy with his head on my lap is curiosity about life. And too, I am talking trust, even love.

All morning Sean keeps coming to me, really good-natured, wanting to play. That is, wanting me to play with him.

I am busy with Terri and tell Sean I can't play just now. Bob tries to get Sean's attention but he is not interested.

Later that day we are all on the playground. I look for Sean and find him furiously flapping the ground behind the large crawling tunnel. He is sobbing. I go to him and he gets up to run away. I call for him not to go.

He stops and turns toward me. As I approach him he runs to me and almost leaps into my arms. I kneel to hold him and he is still sobbing audibly, his thin body shaking. He clutches me tightly.

I walk, holding him, trying to console him. We walk and

walk. He is trembling. I take him back inside and he runs behind
the chair in the corner, curling himself into a ball, whining. He
tries to crawl beneath the wall ventilator, tightly covering his eyes
with his fists.

I stay with him, always touching him. I talk about the fright
and fear he must feel but I do not know what it is about. I stay
with him, talking and touching him through it, and Sean calms. I
ask him to look at me and he does, briefly, with reddened swollen
eyes. I say that I hope he is okay now. He breathes more easily,
regularly. I say how about lunch, and he gets up and we go eat
together.

I realize I did not register how special it was for Sean to
approach me, did not register his fragility for rejection.

Reading Sean is a mystery. Reaching him is an unceasing
effort. Engaging him is yet another realm of struggle. There is
virtually no reciprocation. He is comfortable only in his solitude,
his repetitive infantilisms.

I choose to reach Sean through the constancy of my
presence. I am choosing to engage him through sheer physical
patterning, having him do things he does not do of his own
initiative, taking him through the motions of a larger experience
than mere compliance. And I play with him.

Through play I establish myself as an undeniable presence,
not entirely of his making, one outside of his control. Play is
contact, seductive, intensive, purposeful contact. My play with
Sean is highly intimate, intrusive, physical, sensory contact. And
he responds with abandon.

Sean's eyes are bright and focused and sparkling, looking
easily at me. He gives the sign for up. I lie on my back, knees
bent to my chest, stockinged feet perpendicular to the floor. Sean
approaches so his belly rests against my feet; I take his
outstretched hands in mine and raise him above my head like an
airplane.

And he used to be terrified of this.

Now he loves it. He lets Bob play with him too, tickling,
pummeling, kneading. Even Mara. Sean comes alive here in a way

so out of character with his usual attitude and deportment. His look is clear, direct. His laughter is deep and rippling and so much like a little boy. And his abandon, so unlike his typically guarded, obscured demeanor.

We take a leisurely drive to the beach. The waves are big and pounding, churning up lots of white foam that floats onto the shore. Thick, fluffy stuff, perfect to blow and flap.

I keep interrupting Sean. I want him to open to something different. I get him to kick a ball as we run along the lapping tide. We kick it through the thin layer of water, kick it through the mounds of foam. Sean enjoys it, the sprays of water, the exploding foam.

On the way back we stop to take a short canoe ride in the waterway. Sean is eager to get in the boat, but once we start gliding along he resumes his air of casual indifference.

"Hey Sean, this is pretty magical. Look! We're floating on the water! Floating!"

He reaches over the side and flaps the velvety surface a couple of times to show me he heard. No big deal.

One day Sean arrives with a swollen cheek. I check it out and, although he is reluctant, he lets me. Looks like a tooth has severely abscessed.

I call Joan and she is surprised. She has not noticed anything. She agrees to my suggestion to take him to a dentist and politely refuses my offer to go with them. Hasn't noticed?

A couple of days later Sean has the tooth extracted. When I next see him, the cheek is still a bit swollen and he lets me look in his mouth. His gums are inflamed, raw. Throughout the entire affair he has scarcely shown any discomfort or pain. It had to hurt him. A true stoic.

6

Approaching Communication

Hah, that's the ticket, don't talk to anybody . . . open your mouth, and they'll step on you.
Language? Language?
Speak? Speak? About what?

Celine

"Sean. Do this." I put my hands on my head.
He puts his hands on his head. Looking at me.
"Do this." I pull my ears outward.
He does. No expression.
"Do this." Open my mouth wide and extend my tongue.
He does.

Whatever gestures and grimaces, postures and contortions I do, Sean will follow. He easily understands and complies with the game of imitation, and even seems to like it. Probably he enjoys seeing me act entirely silly.

In this process I introduce several fundamental hand gestures from sign language. Eat. Drink. Toilet. Walk. From time to time I show the sign associated with what we are doing or about to do and say the word with it. Play. Up, for when Sean does the airplane on my feet. He readily repeats the simple hand movements and sometimes attempts a sound similar to the word, usually an explosive consonant. "Puh!" "Kuh!" "Tuh!"

More and more I couple the sign with the word, the sign with the action. I am moving it to another level. I am putting Sean in situations to reveal an understanding, a comprehension, and make an autonomous choice.

I am sitting at the table with several pieces of an apple I am using to coax Michael. Sean saunters over, calmly and directly staring at the apple. Quickly, he snatches a piece and eats it. I tell him it is not his to take, that he should ask if he wants one. Unabashedly he takes another. I tell him again, more sternly.

He pulls a chair up next to me, close to the apple slices. He stares at them. I resume working with Michael and Sean tries to stealthily sneak a few pieces. I tell him to put them back, which he does.

Bob calls him away from the table, to come and play. Sean gets up and wanders around, whining, very agitated. Bob asks what's wrong and Sean takes Bob's hand, walks to the table and puts it on the apples. Bob says they are not his to take and Sean needs to ask me for them.

Sean looks at me with a glare, angry, and walks away.

In the course of our play, Sean regularly makes a variety of sounds and noises, spontaneously and expressively.

"Leedle-leedle-leedle," he says.

I repeat, "Leedle-leedle-leedle."

"Eeeeeeeeee," says Sean "Laaallll-aaaa-llll."

And so do I. In the texture and flow of play I imitate his sounds just as I may imitate his gestures or postures, a context of casual but almost continual vocalizations, of movements and relaxation and laughter and looking and touching. And I notice that Sean makes all the sounds and mouth positions and articulations necessary for speech.

As we play I match his changing patterns, which become a kind of singing together. Sometimes I vary the pitch or rhythm or volume and Sean similarly shifts with me, sometimes exchanging roles, leading and following and harmonizing, back and forth. I play with my voice, my sounds, and I play with his, looking in the mirror or his head on my stomach, cupping my hands over his ears, opening and closing, putting his hand to my throat, his hand to his own chest, my palm on and off his mouth. As play, we explore the nature and fun of sound, of making sounds. But sound as speech is another matter.

"Leedle-leedle-leedle," Sean says.
"Leedle-leedle-leedle," I go.
Then, "Sean, do this: leedle-leedle-leedle."
He just looks at me.

Holding his hand to my throat. "Mmmmmmmm."
Then I put his hand on his own throat. Silence.
I puff out a candle. "Buh!" "Puh!"
Sean's turn. He whooshes it out like blowing bubbles.
Looking in the mirror together. "Sean, do this: Ahhh! Oooo!"
He imitates my mouth movements but no sound.
He seems so confused. Appears to try so hard, intently watching me, but it is as if he cannot make it all work inside.
I keep at it. It is loaded, and I am touching something.

"Sean, look." I make a facial expression.
He imitates quickly and looks away.
"Sean, do this." I pucker my mouth round in a circle. "Oooooo."
He contorts his face, opens his mouth wide. "Aaaaaa!" looking abruptly away.
In the mirror together, I say, "Do this: tuh! tuh! tuh!"
He explodes, "Buh!" while turning away.

Sean makes an expression or motion or sound other than the one I make. And sooner or later ends up making every expression, motion, or sound I have asked, but never when I ask it.

This sound making as precursor to speech is an intense, complex, sensitive, powerful affair for Sean. Face-to-face, with unwavering eyes, he convincingly fumbles to repeat a syllable that I have heard him make many times, he strains and grimaces to imitate a sound pattern that he freely sings. I look into his eyes and I do not know if it is volitional or if his brain is not synchronizing. Or if the emotional significance of learning to

speak is so deep and volatile and convoluted that it makes both of
these suspicions true.

For Sean to speak would make him more of this shared
world, and for some reason I feel that he really does not want that,
not now, that his distance and his difference have a sense and
meaning that he is not ready to give up. Here he is, after nine
years, and if anything is obvious it is that Sean has no desire to
communicate any differently than before. Sean does not need to
speak. Moreover, has no intention to.

We come back from a long, hot, exhausting walk and I sit
at the table to write. I notice Sean wandering around, ripe for
some favorite pastime, so I give him some chalk and go to the
blackboard to get him started. He haphazardly scratches around
with the chalk and I return to my writing. Soon enough, I hear the
telltale puffing and Sean is crouching on the floor, fanatically
blowing clouds of colored chalk dust. I tell him to quit it, to use
the chalk on the board or leave it alone. He leaves it alone, sulking
over to the armchair and flopping into it with the large stuffed
lion. Again a familiar sound interrupts me and Sean is salivating
and licking the fur on the lion. He sees me looking and he stops.
I tell him he can play with the lion but not to spit on it. He throws
it behind the chair and sits staring at me. I continue writing and
unwrap a new package of paper from the cellophane.

Cellophane!

Within seconds Sean is next to me, hungrily eyeing the
wrapping. Trying to ignore him, I toss it in the trash can. He goes
for it. I hesitate a bit, tired of being on his case, but then tell him
to put it back. He does, staying close by. I go back to writing and
before long I hear the loud crinkling of the cellophane. All right,
I think, I will let him keep it and maybe he will surprise me. He
walks around and sits on the floor behind me. Silence. I turn, and
Sean is assiduously pressing his soft, pink tongue on the
cellophane stretched between his fingers. I tell him to throw it
away. Immediately he begins flapping vigorously on the
cellophane, making a loud, high-pitched "EEEEEEEE!" I say
again for him to throw it away and we will find him something
else to do. Abruptly, he rises and runs to the trash can, puts in the

wrapping, runs back to me and looks straight into my eyes with the piercing "EEEEEEE!" and starts flapping me repeatedly and forcefully on the top of my head. I am shocked at both his assertiveness and the intensity of his flapping. I grab his hands and tell him to stop, that it hurts me. I say I know he is angry at me but he is not to hit me. As I let go of his hands he begins again. He is furious. "EEEEEEE!" I flap his head back, saying that it hurts. "EEEEEEE!" he wails and flaps my head even more.

I take his hands and stand up, and he begins crying, sobbing. He is extremely worked up. I hold him to my side and tell him we will walk. We go outside and I hold him closely as we walk around and around, and I talk about his anger, about my wanting him to stop his compulsions, about his making choices. Gradually, he calms, we return inside, and he leaves for the day.

He has never expressed himself so clearly and so directly. Something is happening.

For months I have studied and pondered just what Sean's message is. I continually found him saying that he is indifferent to people, bitterly, deeply, caustically indifferent. He has learned to keep them away, even as they keep trying to find a way in. And so, in a very real sense, Sean has learned a powerful control.

Something was happening for Sean to display such anger at me, and I strongly suspect it is not simply because I have continually frustrated his efforts. Not at all, because time after time, if there is any chance at a battle of wills, of who could best incite whom to levels of intolerance, Sean has already proven himself consistently equal if not superior to me.

Sean's anger here is a message. A message that says he is not indifferent to me, that I affect him. That maybe I am finding a way in, maybe he is letting me in, and he is angry, he is frightened. At me. And at himself.

7

Personality

It is a very funny situation. We know the behavior of an electron is not completely determined by the laws of physics. You believe that the behavior of a human being is completely determined by the laws of physics. Electrons are unpredictable, people are predictable. And you call this psychology.

Arthur Koestler

You do not expect much of an infant. An infant is pampered, indulged. Communication is constantly interpreted from minimal cues, gestures, sounds, looks.

Left to himself, Sean would remain securely and comfortably within his infantilism. But infancy is also fragile, and Sean is so convincing. I am reluctant to push too hard, to shatter what has served him. Yet it is this that shelters him and prevents any initiative for change. I look beyond this role of his to the more solid person Sean suggests.

I impose my presence upon him, a presence at once deliberate, precise, sustained. And I shatter him.

Sean's response is to accommodate, which is a miracle of sorts, proving he is paying attention. If his infantilism and his patterns of weirdness are any kind of fortress they are more to keep people out than they are some inherent, vital necessity he must maintain. Perhaps a sanctuary, perhaps a shelter.

But his weirdness has not been defense enough in the face of my intent and perseverance. I know now that Sean can respond, react, reveal, can comprehend and even communicate where he could not—or would not—before.

Yet I now also question how much of what I know is

actually Sean and how much is because I have set it up. I have pushed, leaned on him, relentlessly. Surrounding, prodding, immersing, flooding Sean with events and situations and choices that are entirely outside the range of his experience. And he adapts. He alters the seeming rigidity of his patterns according to how I press him.

His gloved responses neatly fit the hand of my requests. Pushing a thing only reveals how yielding, or resistant, it may be. It says nothing about what inherently moves it. And in this, motivations emerge. I want to know what motivates Sean.

One morning Sean comes in and goes directly to the large pillows on the carpet, hiding under them. He is very worked up. I go and sit with him, stroking his back, talking, trying to console him. He does not pull away but does not calm down at all. I think to involve him in something and say for him to sit at the table with me while I do some writing, giving him a pencil and paper. He ignores it and really works into a frenzy. I'm groping for some way to deal with it. I get us some juice, which does nothing. He does not even look at it. Sean it truly upset, crying and squirming about and fiercely rubbing his eyes with his fists.

I entreat him to show me what is wrong, to show me what I can do to help. He just sobs pathetically. I stand up and tell him to come with me and we walk outside. He remains agitated as we walk around the field under the trees, so I take him to my car and we get inside, closing the doors. I do not know why, but I sense that somehow being contained would be comforting to him. I keep touch with him, my hand on his shoulder or knee, and as I talk he calms a little. After awhile I ask if he would like to walk some more and he opens the car door and gets out. We walk and I talk about how difficult it must be for him at his home, how nobody knows what to do with him and how he does not know what to do with them. How awkward and uncomfortable and lonely and even ugly it must be.

As I talk Sean looks at me intently and finally, for the first time in over two hours, he is calmed down.

I back up.

My focus is not overtly on Sean, even though I am as saturated as ever with awareness of him virtually every instant. I disrupt the routine, which was routineless but beginning to sniff of regularity, familiarity. I am not *on* Sean continually. The flow is more random, sometimes having a session for comprehension or signing, sometimes calling to him for play. At other times I leave a vacancy, a space for him to act within.

My first surprise is that he does not fill this space with his things. Any flapping or blowing he does is incidental, casual, without any of the former absorption and tenacity.

My next surprise is how social Sean is. He initiates where he never did. If I am writing, he takes the pencil away and sits on my lap, grinning, wanting to play. He pulls the pillow from under Bob's head while he's reading and giggles. Terri becomes a victim of Sean's spontaneous attacks with a gleam and cunning and humor that go far beyond simple interference. In the midst of Terri's drawing one of his fascinating and elaborate creations on the chalkboard Sean calmly walks up and erases it. Which drives Terri into fury while Sean ripples with laughter.

Sean is really with us, in contexts that display a true personality, a humming little child who is alert and responsive and comprehending and good natured.

I was not expecting this much.

Of course nothing is clear and smooth and dramatically obvious.

We all take a leisurely walk through a park. Terri and Sean go ahead of Bob and me, holding hands and seeming to enjoy each other's company—a really nice scene. A while later Terri walks back to join us, but no Sean. We tell Terri to go get him. He goes, but comes back alone. We continue walking and come across Sean, stripped to his underpants, bent over a rain puddle and covered with wet mud. He looks at us, delighted, returning to his graceful, practiced flapping of the puddle's thin, gleaming surface.

Another day in the room. I can tell that Sean really needs to use the bathroom but I am not going to interpret his subtle looks and movements for him. I keep writing at the table while he frantically paces and makes little whimpering noises.

"Hey Sean, relax. How about writing on the chalkboard with Terri?"

He whines and goes toward the board but does not take any chalk, keeps on pacing. I am careful not to ask what's up, what he wants. He goes near the door several times as if to leave. Casually, I call him back.

"Sean, don't go. How about getting a magazine? Or you can blow some bubbles if you want."

More whining, on a much higher pitch. Poor kid, he must be about to burst.

It takes over twenty minutes. Sean comes over, looking me straight in the eye and firmly pulls at my hand to get up. He takes me into the bathroom and probably pees a quart.

From time to time I have occasion to encounter a mute person and then I realize just how reliant I am on vocal communication to feel connected with someone. The mute people I know have such a remarkable ease of themselves that I end up feeling somewhat awkward and embarrassed in my wielding about this useless speaking. Still, I find there is an undeniable connection with them outside of speech.

Only when I met Sean did I fully realize how much this sense of connectedness relies not necessarily on speech, not on listening, not even on eye or body contact. There is an essence, a desire, an intent that is recognized, almost tangible, which opens a person to connect with another. When I met Sean he had none of this. I saw nothing familiar, nothing recognizable to connect with.

Now, I am beginning to.

Yet I wonder if what I am seeing is actually newness and change, or instead, a more complete portrayal that Sean is more comfortable to display, his truer self.

I pick Sean up at his house to go the zoo and I know that something is different. He is so animated, really delighted to see me. Joan even comments that he actually acted like he has been waiting for me to arrive. Sean gestures hello, taking my arm and putting it across his shoulders while he holds me around my waist. As we leave Joan says goodbye and Sean seems to ignore her. She gives him a kiss on the cheek and a hug, stiff and flat. She is clearly awkward. I catch a glimpse of Sean caught between two roles: his infantilism, dependencies, and isolation with his family, and this demonstrative, beginning emergence with me.

He takes in the zoo pretty casually. I stop at a particular cage and point out the animals and he points back. I tell him bits of information about them, the tiger, the ocelot, the monkeys, alligators, snakes. Nothing special.

We get to the petting area with the domesticated animals and now he is excited. Some geese catch his attention and he approaches them. They waddle away, honking loudly. Sean laughs, looks at me as if to share the humor, and continues to stalk the geese, tentatively but persistently until they find refuge in some dense bushes. Close by he sees a large aviary filled with colorful, chattering birds, hopping and flying, and watches, fascinated, making all sorts of noises almost to mimic the birds or attract their attention.

As the day passes Sean becomes quite spirited, wanting to hold my hand, grinning and looking often at me. He climbs up my back and sits on my shoulders. He runs ahead of me, looking back and smiling, as if trying to get me to chase him. We eat lunch and rest awhile under the flowering trees and watch the peacocks, with Sean still in an alert and good-natured mood.

On the drive back Terri is sitting quietly and contented. He is neatly, rather primly dressed and Sean starts to play with him, pulling his shirt from his pants and tickling his stomach. Never has Sean been so assertive. Terri begins to get upset, tucking his shirt back in only to have Sean pull it out and tickle him, laughing. Poor Terri gets more agitated and worked up to the point that he screams, tantrumlike, and then breaks down crying. Sean stops abruptly. He drops his grin, showing real concern for Terri, resting his hand on Terri's leg. Sean reaches over and with the back of his hand gently touches Terri's cheek, now wet with tears.

I retain this image of a suddenly alive, alert, compassionate boy while I arrange a session with Sean for some basic comprehension, playing with colored Cuisenaire rods. He becomes convincingly inert, retarded, dull. I give up. He gets on the bus and I happen to see him, seated next to a window, salivating and pressing his tongue against the glass. Thick-lidded eyes, idiot-looking. I stand outside the bus to wave goodbye with his face inches before me and he acts—or is—wholly oblivious. He leaves in a cloud of smelly black diesel.

8

Forcing Issues

From far back he remembered being driven into secrecy because whatever he revealed seemed to arouse disapproval or punishment.

Ursula LeGuin

I continue to entreat Jeff and Joan to become involved in the process I am developing. They show no interest or desire.

With Sean they are embarrassed, disappointed, exasperated. While I regard these changes in Sean as an emergence and, more significantly, an indication of his capabilities, his parents give me the impression that this awakening, this coming out of Sean, means only more problems. In their speech, their body language, their avoidance and excuses, they effectively distance themselves from responsibility, from being part of this complex weaving.

They talk of "Sean-Sean" as if he is unfairly held within this protracted infancy as a quirk of biology or biochemistry, awaiting release by the correct miracle catalysis. Blame simmers within them over the scores of failures, the attempts they hoped would work this release but did not. I am seeing the disappointment begin to cloud over into resentment toward me, whenever I do catch a glimpse of their eyes.

Sean is jealous.

He does not mind when Bob and I talk but if I spend time with Terri, he sulks, whines, walks restlessly about.

I am sitting at a table talking with Mara and Sean is

agitated. He suddenly walks up behind me and grabs my head between his hands, squeezing hard, making a guttural sound of frustration and anger. I am shocked and I turn to face him.

"Sean, hey, I know you are upset with me but I want to talk with Mara."

He looks me straight in the eyes, taking the sides of my face in his hands and pinches my temples, restrained but quite forceful. He is enraged.

I take his hands down. "Don't do that. It hurts."

In our early play sessions I would put my mouth to his nose, telling him to relax as he nervously pushed at me, and gently gnaw at it.

Before I can say anything else Sean leans forward and firmly, mockingly bites my nose and walks away.

His energy is bursting, in such contrast to the listless indifference that used to characterize him. His clarity grows, his alertness, attentiveness, expressiveness, even enthusiasm.

And as he gives more I want still more.

Before lunch, I ask Sean what he wants to do. He makes a quick gesture with his hand and turns away. I tell him I like him to show me what he wants, that I like to look at someone when I talk with them. He walks away, sulking and pouting. He hides where I cannot see him. I wait.

Soon he comes to me, looking in my eyes, and makes some feeble signs with his hand several times. Calmly, directly, with a deeply sincere look. I show him the correct sign for "Eat." Still looking at me, he easily signs correctly. We go to lunch.

Later that afternoon, Bob goes into the bathroom and finds Sean standing in the toilet stall, urinating deliberately on the paper roll.

My every instant is one of vigilance.

My time is constant with scrutiny, evaluation, reassessment.

The moment, the power, the meaning is in the interaction. It is always and only the interaction.

Sean comes in a good mood, eyes sparkling. He wants to

play. I greet him, rustle him up a bit, and tell him I am busy with Terri right now but I will be finished in a few minutes and then we can do something. He waits, kind of hanging around.

As soon as I get up from playing with Terri, Sean goes across the room and begins spitting on the floor, flapping and blowing it.

I feel a game coming on.

I tell him I would like to play if he does.

He moves away where I cannot see him, and I hear him spit, then flapping and blowing. I again say I would like to play.

No change.

Then I say I don't want him to be hidden, that I want him to be with us.

Abruptly, Sean becomes very agitated and gets up, whimpering. He climbs some shelves, crying. He stops and spits, flapping furiously. He throws off all his clothes with a sudden sardonic laugh.

He definitely catches me off guard. On one hand I feel he did this to ensure my attention, escalating to the point of forcing me to respond. But on the other hand I think that this is somehow a parody of his life, to guarantee my disapproval and even rejection. Something much more familiar to him than acceptance.

From seemingly simple episodes explode a trying ordeal. I am baffled. He seems so calculating, cunning, intentional.

For several days I have given Sean a set of Cuisenaire rods at a table for him to explore, to play with. He kind of shuffles them around but nothing is focused or deliberate. I sit with him from time to time, sometimes just being with him, sometimes arranging the wooden rods into patterns by color or length, side by side or standing them on end. Sean casually watches, doing nothing until I direct him

I want to involve him as well as to confirm what I suspect he easily can do. I stack some rods of progressively shorter lengths, making a stair-stepped pyramid. Sean watches. I repeat it several times and the table is scattered with pyramids. I begin another and, after a few rods, I hand the next one to Sean. He just holds it. Silently, I open my hand and he gives it to me. With precise and exaggerated flourish I place the rod on the stack, then hand it back to Sean. I make a sweeping, inviting gesture to the unfinished stack. Looking at me with wide, innocent eyes, he just holds it.

I repeat my demonstration, but after handing him the rod I now point to the place on the stack and say, "Sean, look, it goes right here."

He puts it on the table next to the stack.

"No," I say, again pointing to the top of the stack, "put it here."

Poker-faced, he places it behind the stack.

Of course, I suspect something. Days later I try again.

I put all the rods on the table in a random pile. I take the longest one and lay it in front of us, saying the color, then the next longest, and so on, until all ten lengths of differing color are placed next to one another in sequence. I then imitate the pattern immediately beneath it, placing a colored rod against its match. I talk it through.

"What's next? A red one. Let's look for a red one."

After a couple of sequences, I ask Sean to pick out the next rod. "Okay, how about a yellow one."

He picks a green one.

I look at him. He looks back, unblinking.

"Nope. We need a yellow one. Just like this guy." If there is any doubt, I point to the yellow rod in the upper arrangement.

He picks a black one.

"Nope."

He picks out every color except yellow.

Next day at the table, same set-up. I try to be casual and cheerful but we both sense a showdown. I pick an arrangement from the piled rods.

"Okay, it's your turn."

I watch Sean almost touch the first correct rod with his hand but quickly, deftly pick another. We are sitting beside one another, our chairs almost touching.

Immediately, forcefully I shout "NO!"

He is startled. I have never shouted this way before. He puts the rod down. Calmly, I repeat the color that is next.

He goes for another. As he touches it, again, "NO!"

Each time Sean picks an incorrect color and each time I shout vehemently. The tension mounts. It is severely trying, neither of us giving in. Sean begins to cry softly.

I feel terrible doing this. But somehow I feel I must see it through. Sean's signals are paradoxical, because if he were genuinely distressed or truly did not want to do any of this I know he could find a way out. He is resisting, but he is staying with it.

He could pick the rods entirely by chance.

He does not have to pick any at all.

Sean is showing that he understands but does not want to reveal it. I am sweating, my pulse pounding. Sean is crying as he reaches for another color. "NO!" I shout. Inside I plead with him. Why?

I keep pushing. And Sean is pushing back. Not hiding, not running away, not avoiding or slipping out of it. The air is heated. The strain is volatile.

Sean picks up a rod.

"NO!"

And suddenly he reaches directly for the correct one, tears streaming down his cheeks, and places it down. Smoothly, without hesitation he picks out the next one, then the next. He completes the sequence. He has looked down at the table the entire time, crying.

I say quietly to do it again.

He does.

Again.

After arranging five sequences without a moment of reluctance or hesitation Sean looks up at me, eyes puffed from tears but steady, and signs. "Eat, drink, walk."

And we do.

I know now that confronting Sean is like trying to compress hot mercury between my palms. It is clearly easier to leave him alone. But I don't. I saw something, partly because I sensed it and pushed but also because Sean let me. He let me see.

So I am thanking him. We are sitting together on the rug next to the window. It is a cold, clear day.

I tell Sean that living with his family must be very difficult for him, not really trusting, not being trusted. That he must be terribly lonely not to open to anyone.

He is being cool, looking out at the sky, doodling with some fluff on the rug.

I tell him he is proud, strong, intelligent, sensitive. That he is beautiful and special and that I respect him. I say that to give up his act does not mean giving himself up. To make choices that are good for him will not leave him without power but will make him stronger and more free.

Without looking, he reaches over and covers my mouth with his hand.

I move it gently away. "I know you don't want to hear this."

He turns to look at me. With both his hands he covers my eyes.

I interpret Sean's growing animation, initiative, and general ease as letting himself trust me.

He comes in Monday morning eager and responsive. His face and arms are covered with small open sores that he has picked raw. The previous Friday, Joan had picked him up and the tension from her was noticeable. I try to imagine what goes on between them and cannot help but fill with pity for Sean.

He and I go for a walk and Kathy joins us. As Kathy and I talk, Sean picks up his pace and moves ahead. I call him back, saying I like him to be with us. He stands looking forward and waits woodenly.

As Kathy and I resume talking he is again moving ahead. I say to him I know he is mad that I am talking with Kathy but I like him and want him around. Nothing to make a big deal over.

Kathy then tells Sean she likes him too. And doesn't he like her?

Sean grunts. Walks faster, then runs.

Kathy calls to him.

Nothing.

I call and he immediately runs back, burying his head into me. "Sean, I know it's hard dealing with a new person. I spend time with you, and I spend time with other people. Kathy is a good person and we can be with her together. She won't just go away."

Kathy kneels down beside him. "Sean, don't you like me?"
Sean turns his head and spits directly in her face.

9

Power Plays
and Parents

They each disapproved of each other. My father especially
disapproved of my mother; the net effect was to confuse me.

Edmund White

After all the time I have spent with Sean, I want some insights into
the impact, if any, at his home. I try and try to arrange meeting
with Jeff and Joan and realize they are stalling. So I virtually
badger them continually until one afternoon Joan agrees to talk
with me. Jeff says he cannot make it.

Joan arrives with her mother, whom I have never met. Joan
is clearly nervous and evasive, constantly looking to her mother
who is quick to take over, combative and domineering. She knows
Sean-Sean, she commands to me, and her portrayal of him is of an
infantile and destructive child that shatters any attempts at normal
family life.

I direct my questions at Joan, to pull at her own feelings
and perceptions, but only find a slipperiness, parroting agreement
with her mother. Joan shows herself as a woman tired and
resigned to her fate. Her mother shows herself as angry and
hostile.

Things have certainly turned around from my initial
meetings when Joan was eager for my ideas and objectives, when
she and Jeff agreed to work with me.

Now, as we talk, it is I who does not know the real Sean,
know that he has gotten steadily worse. I am told that I do not

understand, that something is wrong with Sean. Joan knows. She has studied, she is involved with organizations, she has been to numerous professionals.

As we talk, I do know.

I know this is a dead end for Sean. With these people, he has no chance to be anything else.

So I abruptly ask Joan if she and Jeff still want Sean.

Joan's mother is shocked. Yet, evenly, looking at me directly, Joan says that she and Jeff have been discussing for some time whether to place Sean somewhere. She discloses that they have been arguing heatedly over it.

I say that it would greatly clarify my role if they resolve their decision. I would be better able to look into placement for Sean than to work under the illusion that his home life is stable. I say, above all it would be fairer to Sean not to be living with such ambiguity.

Joan agrees. Her mother sits tight-lipped.

After they leave I am in a turmoil, drained.

As I intrude more upon Sean, demand more from him, I learn more about him as he changes. But my understanding continually shifts with the differing perspectives I get. I am so restricted in knowing him because his world is so hidden, his inner truths and feelings that I can only interpret, decipher, or intuit. It is so fundamentally difficult to know Sean, this child, this person, not just because he does not speak, but because he does so very little to communicate at all. I keep returning to see that his world is so raw and bitter upon him.

Following a weekend with his family Sean comes in with a coating, shielded, aloof, arrogant, as if a contrivance within which he fends off the day's assaults. I search his face, his manner, for what it is like for him at his home, what is the ambiance, the essence. For above all, his primary sense of who he is comes from who he is with Jeff and Joan, how they see him, react to him, are with him.

Repeatedly, within the sequence and context of Sean and I together are the stops, the deliberate tugs and testings. The exercise of will and power, as if that is the way, ultimately, to know a sense of self.

I know he wants to walk with Bob and Kathy and Terri and me, but he holds out, not signing. Sarcastic in his deadpan earnestness of signing everything except "Walk," a mockery. With a sigh, I sit down to wait him out and tell everyone to go on—quickly, he signs "Walk" to me. I tell him that everyone wants to know what he wants. He acts entirely flustered and incapable. Again, I tell the others to go ahead and then Sean signs clearly and directly to them.

Whatever it is, get the box, put on the shirt, can suddenly be a stop. My expectations are now far beyond checking for what he understands, rote responses to calculated questions, because I no longer have doubt. I know he knows. And he knows I know, and his stopping no longer has the power it once did with me, and still does with everyone else.

Sean stops, because by staying with the flow, by showing a series of choices and understandings he becomes part of it, but also gives something up, gives in. Perhaps too big a piece of himself. I expect the flow with him in the same way I do with any person, a sharing of connection, of intelligence and humor and feelings, of dignity and respect. That may well be too much for him to handle, to see himself that way.

Deep, piercing exchanges between our eyes. He touches the box, puts on the shirt, giving in, looking at me, crying, crying. I assure him, embrace him. He has such pain, so deep! "Sean," I say, "I really like you, I care for you." He begins to weep, anguished, agonizing.

His stops.
They are making sense.
Lovers that fight only to make up to fight again.
Jeff and Joan and Sean caught in webs of history and intense, competing emotions.
Disappointment, guilt, anger, frustration.
Helplessness, fear, anxiety, hurt.
The righteousness of these emotions, righteous in large part

because of their intensity, in large part because they are the only way to express across whatever holds them as husband, father, son, wife, mother. Whatever holds them by obligation, by projected identity, by thwarted love.

Caught in the web, of starts, trying to make sense of the connection, of what seems to be a connection, then snagged by the confusion. A stop.

It is often easier to find an argument than to resolve one. Like a schoolyard fight, once the first shoulder is shoved. If Sean has not seen reconciliation, has not known affirmation of love, if what he knows is minefields of conflict and posturing and confusion and distancing, his stops make sense. Perfect sense.

One afternoon, I am surprised when Jeff shows up unannounced. I have never talked alone with him. Sean has already left.

We shuffle around some male talk, finding a small safe spot of common ground. He is about my age, close to the same height but he is decidedly more muscular—I recall seeing some bench weights at their house—with closely cropped hair, tightly fitting clothes, tensed jaw, thick, strong hands. An economy of movement and facial expression, playing it close to the chest, in vigilant control. Within all this I sense a burdened, sad, troubled man—and a fuse about to run out at any time, primed for explosion.

We sit down and I wait. I know whatever he offers will be more revealing and genuine than if I probe. He begins to speak, in measured phrases, thick, blunt pieces that break off with pained difficulty from the mountain of thought and feeling inside, as if he wants to unload. It is exceedingly hard for him. He stares fixedly at a place on the ground between us. His slow, serious phrasing is followed by long and protracted pauses, searching, awkward.

Awkward, I sense, because he seldom, likely never, has been so open. He appears to be searching, to formulate and clarify what he probably has not previously allowed himself to look at with such directness.

He reveals a man heavy from brooding and resignation, caught in a life that offers little comfort, full of shattered dreams.

He sees with precision how Sean is the scapegoat for the resentment and disillusion and frustration that need somewhere to go. He sees Joan's dominance, wielding a power against which he struggles, against a tone of her constant dissatisfaction and disappointment. He has distanced himself from Sean, knowing he could not be the father he imagined wanting to be, just as Sean could not ever be the son. But the resentment and disillusion and frustration remain, boiling, and the only expression of it is to scapegoat. Or to explode.

He describes, in admission, his trouble with alcohol. Of hitting Sean.

He pauses, faltering. Clenching and releasing his fists, he burns a hole in the ground with an unfocused stare.

Then, allusions to episodes of rage, overwhelmed with futility, gone for days at a time. He has grown afraid of himself. He wants to stay distanced from his son, stay removed, because of that fear. But Sean unerringly gets to him, and he is still afraid.

So he does not spend much time at home, putting in a lot of overtime and pursuing his favorite hobby of photography. He lights up, his eyes darting about the room as he talks of his desire to establish himself professionally, particularly for photographing race cars. He says he has not had a drink for a long time. After a prolonged silence, where I see him wrestling something around inside, he looks up.

I am surprised at his candor as he meets my eyes and says that he understands what I am doing with Sean. He has watched how the many other specialists did nothing more than hold Sean at arm's length and describe what they saw. Yes, he understands what I am doing, he says, and he believes in it. And he does hear me insisting I cannot do it alone, that he and Joan need to involve themselves. He knows that, too.

As much as he believes all this, he says he cannot do it. He cannot do it because Joan refuses the possibility that the way Sean is has something to do with them. She refuses it so vigorously—and I envision the nasty scenes of screams and accusations, and know undoubtedly that Sean listens in the other room—she has threatened to leave. And he cannot do it because he simply has exhausted himself.

Jeff agrees that they should decide if Sean would be better off somewhere else, with a foster family, in an adopted home, even a residential facility. It would be fairer to Sean and easier for his family than to prolong this ambiguity. And, though painfully difficult, they need to face the truth. Yet here again Jeff must stand up to Joan because she does not want to give Sean up. Once more I imagine the scenes as they argue. And I imagine Sean. I no longer wonder why he is so hardened, and why he is so reluctant to let me reach him inside.

Jeff gets ready to leave. I tell him he is welcome at any time, to see what I am doing or just to talk. He thanks me. It is understood that he will try again with Joan about placing Sean, despite how hard it is. I see him here desperately afraid, of her, of himself.

After Jeff leaves I sit with the flood of it all rushing within me and I realize I never once saw him smile.

Sean does not see me as I watch him walking up the ramp.

There is such a change from this same boy of several months ago who would creep tentatively, timidly beside the wall, appearing helpless and afraid, pulling his jacket up to cover his head. Now here he is walking confidently and easily along with the flow of the other children, an open carefree expression on his face. As he so often does, he rhythmically taps the railing with the backs of his fingers while he walks.

The instant he sees me I greet him, and he transforms into his persona of indifference and aloofness.

I want Sean to communicate directly and assertively from his wants and needs, and not just in response to my intrusions. More and more I am seeing his cycles of deliberate contrivance alternate with a naturalness and trust. As if to check out, to test what will work with me and what will not, as if to struggle with his own choices of how to be.

Bob and I talk about what to do this morning. The boys are active and alert and the atmosphere is easy. How about a walk?

Terri says he wants to go.

We look at Sean. He is spotlighted. He turns his face away,

as if he isn't following what is going on. I back off to give him another opening. To everyone I ask, where do you want to go? Terri says to the park. Bob concurs.

Sean has sauntered around to my side and in my periphery I catch him signing "Walk.""Well," I say to Terri and Bob, "why don't you guys go on. I'd like to go too," I continue, "but I don't know what Sean wants."

They begin to go. I sense Sean moving more anxiously and he stands in front of me, facing me. He looks at me, then averts his eyes to the side and signs for walk.

We are testing each other with split hairs. I do not respond and tell Bob and Terri to go on. They leave and Sean gets very angry, as if he cannot believe I will not let him go. He whines loudly, walking briskly around the room, then runs and collapses on the floor, arms and legs flailing. Crying, he crawls behind a chair, then climbs on top of a cabinet, throwing off all his clothes. I say succinctly to him that this was his choice. He knows what to do, he does not always have to play this kind of game, he does not always have to push. I sit at the table to write.

Terri and Bob return. Sean is still naked atop the cabinet, quietly standing. I realize how often and how easy it is to relate to Sean through some negative interaction, how much he sets it up so there is little other choice.

It is nearly lunchtime. I tell Sean to get down so he can get dressed and clean up to eat. He climbs from the cabinet and puts his clothes on but with his shoes on opposite feet. Lately, as he dresses, Sean has put his shirt on backwards or inside out. I simply sit with him, waiting until he puts it on correctly. He gave that up but now it is the shoe trick. I tell him to sit in the chair until he puts them on right. Bob and Terri go to eat.

Sean looks at me, puppy-eyed, imploring: how could I be so cruel to someone who just doesn't understand? I tell him to knock it off, just put on the shoes so we can eat. He takes them off, turning them over to hold the bottom of each shoe against the bare soles of his feet. Another puppy look. I say it is up to him and I return to my writing.

Off and on, off and on, a dozen times and always on backwards. I feel him drawing my attention, even my anger. He sits looking at me and urinates in his pants. Takes his shoes off and on.

Bob and Terri return from lunch. Sean still sits. Soon it is time to leave, and I say goodbye, see you tomorrow, and follow the boys to the door. Sean shuffles out in his wet pants and backwards shoes.

I see Sean's extremes from natural, unforced openness swinging suddenly to deliberate resistance and defiance, and this shows me the amazing complexity of this boy, the acuity of his perception and the workings of his intellect.

I am continually alert for his attempts at negative encounters, trapping me with irritation and anger and frustration, complex in their meanings and effects. Surely Sean is most familiar with relating this way, ensuring attention. And surely he is expected to be this way, to be a problem. This way, Sean can keep everyone guessing, waiting for the next episode of trouble. He maintains control over his world through his repertoire of created problems that result in his being indulged, acted upon. He evades responsibility and accountability, without ever having to really act for himself, to put out—and certainly without him having to communicate.

As Sean swings erratically and unpredictably with each persona I must be quick to read and anticipate him, to adjust my approaches and reactions. A slow and demanding and sometimes disturbing process. But a process that has evolved, almost dialectically, between us. I know now that Sean is far from the withdrawn , distant, infantile boy I first met. He is unquestionably not the presumably unreachable boy encapsulated in some world of his own. Now, even if negatively motivated, even if erratic and unpredictable, Sean prefers contact, interaction. And he always, somehow, responds.

"Sean, let's paint!"
He walks to the table with casual nonchalance.
"Hey, go put on a painting shirt, remember?"
He just stands there, dumb act.
Christy comes to visit and immediately picks up on the situation. I welcome her and we both put on our cover shirts and

begin to paint. Sean still stands. More visitors come. They all put on shirts and we're having a great time.

"Sean, I'd really like you to paint with us. I know you like it. Why don't you go on and get your shirt?"

He walks to the shelf, reaches directly for a shirt then quickly picks up a small wood block as he turns to look at me. Innocently.

"Aw, Sean, cut it out."

I get up and go into another room with the visitors. When I return Christy is saying to Sean to put on a shirt so he can join her. He walks back to the shelf, picks one up and puts it on. He comes to the table and enthusiastically paints, smearing globs of colors with his brush in a new display of assertiveness. He is really enjoying himself.

His internal wrestling with communicating seems like labor pains.

10

The Outing

How can I justify such an opinion? What scientific evidence can I offer for such an outrageous statement?

R.D. Laing

Sean is very keyed up when Bob and I pick him up at his house. I wonder what his mother might have told him while she packed his things in the small suitcase. Joan is nervous as we load the car, then kisses Sean goodbye and awkwardly tries to embrace him. He just stands indifferently.

We drive to the site down the dirt road, through the sheltering live oaks and the thick stands of palmettos, ending on the beach. We unload the car. Bob will return for us in five days, and I am alone with Sean.

I wanted something dramatic. We will camp on this isolated expanse of beach. I want Sean to come out, even if I have to draw him out.

Within the first hour I am sobered with fear and disbelief that Sean is gone. He is nowhere in sight and dusk is falling. I run along the dunes in a direction I am hoping is his, following what I hope are his footprints. Marshy canals lie beside the dirt roads back to the highway and I am sickened by the thought of Sean's affinity for water.

I had been setting up camp while Sean lay casually in the sand watching me. I sat down to eat some peanuts and he just looked, no gesture or sign. I resumed putting up the tent and Sean began rummaging through the box of food, looking at me. I shook my head No and he flung himself on the sand, angry. Barely a few moments later, while I was arranging things in the tent, I realized that he had run off.

After almost two miles I pause to see a group of houses behind the dunes, then up ahead about a half-mile, some children playing on a shelf of coquina rock jutting into the shoreline. I run along the beach until I am close enough to scan the rocks with binoculars and see that Sean is not among them, so turn back to run to the houses. As I near them, several people are gathered around a sheriff's squad car. My stomach tightens. Then I see Sean sitting in the back seat.

We walk silently back to the campsite and I sort through my feelings: relief, anger, helplessness, shock. I can not afford to underestimate the power of this boy. He has swiftly, deftly evened the arrangement. I look at him, searching his face for clues, a face entirely placid and undaunted, just as he was when sitting in the squad car. All I can do is be honest. I tell him I hope he will not do that again.

He laughs.

I say I was scared to find him gone, that I care for him.

I talk and I feel uneasily that it is somehow clearly his show. As we walk he takes my hand and puts it around his shoulder and tucks his head against my stomach, holding me affectionately around my waist.

I prepare to eat supper with Sean looking at me. He is hungry, holds out his hand, but does not sign. I do not give him any food.

We take a walk in the moonlight, our bare feet in the soft sand while the waves lap against exposed rocks. Sean darts ahead and turns to run down a secluded path, looking back at me. I run to catch up and scold him severely. I tell him my only demand is that he stay always in sight.

I awaken gradually to a peaceful clear morning and to the

reality of where I am, what I am doing with this little boy beside me. Sean is awake with his head covered by his sleeping bag, making tiny sounds and lightly tapping the side of the tent with his fingers. I lie there and imagine Sean was somehow supposed to have changed during the night, that passing through the miracle and mystery of sleep he would awaken cleansed.

We spend our time easily, taking walks, playing together in the water, lying in the warm sand. Often I share his world of silence, or rather, of speechlessness, since the beach is alive with sounds and sensations. The rhythmic lapping of waves and the sucking of the burnt orange coquina sands, the rustling of swaying sea oats, the raucous cries of gulls and the animated scurrying of sandpipers. At other times I talk to Sean, describing, putting words to these displays, keeping a connection between us. On several occasions he comes to me smiling and laughing, to play, climbing on my back or getting me to wrestle.

During a brief rainshower we retreat to the tent and Sean looks at me, signing "Eat," so I give him an apple. This is his first food in twenty-four hours.

Later I fix a meal and eat while Sean watches. He looks at the ground and hesitantly extends his open hand. I stop eating and look at him, waiting. He looks up, turns his head away and signs, "Eat." I resume my meal. In my periphery I see Sean looking at me and signing. As I raise my head to meet his eyes, he stops.

This feels dishonorable, this dehumanizing bribery. I also feel it is all I can do to leverage some change from the tedious impasse we have been in for weeks.

Sean sits, casually blowing sand, then suddenly gets up and walks to me, looking straight in my eyes, signing, "Drink." I give him a large cup of water which he swallows thirstily and he signs again, so I give him another. He drinks this and goes back to sit in the sand, apparently content.

Toward dusk we take a long walk on the beach. Sean stays ahead of me, gradually lengthening our distance and moving closer to the dunes. I feel him testing, pushing the edge. I call to him that I would like us to walk together on the shore. He keeps walking ahead. I call more loudly. Repeatedly. I find myself shouting.

I realize how caught up I am, so negatively drawn in. I sit in the sand, stunned, lost in reflection. Then Sean is sitting beside me, closely. For an indeterminate time I remain deep within my thoughts when he reaches over, touching my mouth gently, turning my face toward him. With a sincere, even concerned look he signs "Play," but I sense it is more to express affection, and I put my arm around him, hugging him to me. He reaches out his arms and hugs in return and we embrace one another, quietly, for awhile. He has pulled me from my mood.

I ask if he is tired. He stands, taking my hand, and leads me to the tent where we soon fall asleep.

Sean sleeps long into the morning. He has urinated in his clothes during the night.

I fix some fruit to eat and Sean whimpers, very agitated, but does not look at me. He is obviously very hungry. He signs for drink with his head turned and I don't respond. Dramatically he throws himself on the ground, crying and wailing. He rolls around in the direction of the food tent and stealthily reaches in. I tell him to cut it out, it won't work. He rolls back away and lies quietly in the sand.

Later in the morning, I lie on my mat to write and Sean comes over and lies full length on my back, his hand resting gently on the back of my shoulders. We are both holding out. By now I am certain he knows I am going for something serious, beyond simply looking for responses which are nothing more than filling in the blanks I provide. Sean knows I am expecting a reaching out of himself, an extension of his being, extending of who he is, a giving. By now I am certain he knows I am as persevering to bring him out as he is tenacious not to come out.

Throughout the day we both remain mute. Sean stays close, lying still and quiet with his head covered with a shirt or towel. From time to time he moves to me, putting my arm around him as he holds me affectionately by my waist. He looks directly at me with a deep, intense, searching gaze.

I wait, I write, I think.

Sean walks up, looks at me and signs for drink. I fill a cup for him and he drains it. He takes my hand and leads me to the stove where the lima beans are cooking. I put a portion into a bowl and wait. He looks at the beans intently. He looks at me, fawnlike eyes, and signs for walk. Then for play. I do nothing. Again, "Walk, Play." He looks down, so I begin to eat from the bowl. He quickly looks up and signs "Eat." I fill another bowl for him and he devours it, then signs for play, followed by a reluctant sign for eat. I give him the remaining beans.

Sean has urinated copiously during the night. I help him rinse his clothes and sheet in the water and hang them over palmettos to dry in the sun. He watches me prepare some fruit and does not sign. I eat while he stares. When I finish I ask him to put his now dry clothes back into the tent and he just looks at me, puppy-eyed. I ask again. He does nothing. Before I know it I am caught up in an intense standoff with Sean easily in control. I walk away feeling drained from futility and frustration. I go for a swim to refresh myself and then lie down on the warm sand. Sean comes and lies close to my side. He puts his arm across my back. Peace is made. I put my hand over his shoulders.

Later, while I am writing, Sean looks and signs for eat and drink. I fix a salad and tea which we eat together. He signs "Eat," still hungry, so I give him an apple and some nuts.

As contrived a situation as this is, something profound is taking place. Sean is likely very angry at the position I have put him in, and it is certainly difficult, exasperating, exhausting, and even disturbing for both of us. But in this arrangement, as tedious and trying is it is, Sean has shown more unmitigated assertiveness, emotion, and above all, more self-generated communication than I have seen in my six months with him. And more than he has ever shown in the past, according to what I have learned about him.

What is happening here defies his history, defies what is assumed about him. It is clear now. Sean is not trapped in some inaccessible interior world. He is acutely aware. Sean is not infantile, feeble, incompetent. He is not mysteriously, weirdly driven by uncontrollable ritual and compulsion. Sean is not out of touch with his feelings and emotions. He is, after all, truly capable of genuine, companionable, expressive communication.

This much I know now, without question. What I do not know is why he does not want to do it.

Supper is cooling and we are both quite hungry after a full day of playing in the sun and sea. Sean signs regularly and we snack on apples and peanuts and water and there is a good feeling between us. He is affectionate and playful, we laugh a lot and are enjoying being together.

The meal is ready and I place two bowls out and fill one, pausing briefly. Nothing. No sign.

I pick up the bowl and begin to eat. Sean signs for drink. It is a ploy, he is not thirsty; he has drunk so much all day he plays with the water I give him. I keep eating. Sean signs. "Play." "Walk." "Drink." He holds out his bowl.

Then, while looking at me, he begins to urinate in his pants as he sits. I shout angrily and abruptly at him to stop, then to go rinse himself in the water. He returns and I start to reprimand him for his games. He looks at me and signs to eat with a barely detectable grin on his face.

I suppose I had romanticized the outcome of this outing into achieving some definitive, dramatic breakthrough. Something as astonishing as Sean suddenly speaking.

Of course, that would be unrealistic and, in fact, oversimplifying the nature of who Sean is and why he is this way. Sean is a constellation of his particular family patterns, individual history, and personal experiences that have shaped his perceptions of himself and the world, shaped the consciousness of his choices. The same processes, in other words, that influence and impact any of our lives. And this makes Sean more similar to most people than, it seems, most people would grant him to be.

Sean is not who he is and does not do what he does because of some singular or traumatic event that made him fundamentally different or immutable or aberrant. His life is a process and an evolution, however idiosyncratic, and not some circumscribed, fixed condition.

I have found Sean to be far more than how his family sees him, and likely more than they want him to be. Far more than has ever been expected from him. Sean is not to be fixed up, made right, cured. Not even changed. He is to be encountered, interacted with, at times confronted, at times encouraged. He is to be reached.

Perhaps not so astonishing, I have found Sean is nothing less than a person. I have affirmed that the power of breakthrough lies in relationship itself versus the efficacy of any treatment.

11

Between Man and Wife

It is better to be alone than to be with someone who doesn't understand you.

Henry Miller

Following the outing we had a week apart in our respective lives. I shaved my beard. Sean has been given an institutional-looking haircut and actually has a little belly on him. I assume he has at least eaten well.

We seem to have emerged into a new arena. Sean carries over an attitude and posture of being very present. He met me solidly during our beach encounter and now seems ready for what is next.

I want to know the options. With Sean, I drive inland to visit two residential programs.

I realize how much I enjoy his company, his alert, peaceful silence. I enjoy giving commentary on the passing landscape as he follows with his eyes and gestures.

This is serious, weighty. Joan and Jeff still vacillate and argue, but I want Sean to know more of the reality being considered. And the reality is thickly sobering and very pathetic. We tour the facilities with a cheerful guide who could be showing off the prize winning gardens of the women's club. Olympic-sized swimming complex, red brick dormitories, spacious cafeteria, manicured grounds. Yet I cannot help but notice, and I know Sean also registers, what is peculiar about the residents and the staff. The roles are clear. To be a resident is to be retarded, and the staff, dressed in impeccable white as that of hospital workers, is to be custodian of these less fortunates. Condescending, patronizing, saccharine-sweet care that differs little whether the resident is eleven or twenty-one.

Do you have any severe problems, I ask.

Occasionally, of course.

And how do you deal with them?

With Sean alongside, the guide, still cheerful, tells me about the restraints, shows us the isolation room, informs with some pride about the resident psychiatric nurse and the facility's well-stocked pharmacy. Thick-lipped, dull-eyed adolescents and adults shuffle in line for lunch, handed to them by the uniformed workers.

I see a small group of young children in a makeshift classroom with a teacher and her assistant. These children are not able to function in the public school, the guide explains, so they stay here while the others are bused into their classes. The teacher seems wholly exasperated. The children sit listlessly, without interest in the mimeographs and plastic toys scattered about. Yes, I find out, they all are medicated. They have to be.

Later, Jeff calls me from work to confirm his agreement to talk with Joan, who is still ambivalent and confused, but more for some encouragement. He asks about the programs and I explain how inadequate they would be for Sean. Jeff sounds somber, joyless, as he thanks me for helping.

In spring, Bob and I take Sean and Terri on a casual three-day camping trip next to a lake. The atmosphere is relaxed. We swim, drift around in the canoe, lie in hammocks during the warm days, tell stories around a fire at night under the dazzling stars.

The simplicity of new experiences, without pressure. The sense of a subtle growth of trust. A mutual trust, as we extend a stronger belief in the capability of these two boys. A belief in the fact of their sheer boyness that they likely may never have been allowed.

I am quite surprised when Sean's parents ask to meet one evening at their house. The atmosphere is grave and stiff as Bob and I seat ourselves. Joan is finishing cleaning up after their supper and Sean is kind of following her around the kitchen. He is in a good mood, giggling and smiling, a contrast to the sullen, forced banter of Joan and Jeff. Sean comes over behind where I am sitting and puts his arms around my shoulders and neck in a hug. I pat on his hands and tell him hello. Jeff is seated on a sofa, facing the television that is loudly on. Joan then settles into a chair opposite Jeff, both of them across the room from Bob and me.

Joan asks Sean to go to his room and, still giggling and smiling, he does. She starts awkwardly to make small talk and as I look at her and Jeff I realize they are oblivious to the television. I excuse myself as I rise and turn it off. The phosphorescent blink seems to startle Jeff from a trance and he stutters through an apology.

The room is tomblike as I speak.

Sean is being put in the middle of some serious emotional pressure, I say, between what I am doing with him and how you treat him at home. You have to decide if you truly still want Sean to live with you as part of your family. If you do, you have to commit yourselves to dealing fairly with him. Any help I can give will work only if you cooperate. Any changes you expect from Sean will only happen out of how you change the way you relate with him. I recognize, of course, how intense and difficult this is to do—but it already is intense and difficult.

I am somewhat shocked as Jeff voices his agreement. He says that Sean is treated like a fixture, an embarrassment, and even worse. Like an untrained pet, an animal. As a family they have an uneasy truce, a facade, acting as if everything is fine, living in bare tolerance of what is not talked about. He admits he has no patience left. He says, looking straight at me, that they should try to find a better place for Sean to live.

Jeff has said all this with directness despite an obvious difficulty in voicing the unspoken. Joan watches him silently yet intently, her body in unmoving, rigid posture. When Jeff finishes he looks down at the floor. The momentary pause is thick, palpable.

Joan speaks, an uncoiling of controlled viciousness. She speaks at Jeff, ignoring Bob and me, going for the throat. She denounces him vehemently, his coldness, his lack of love or caring. The unbearable tension of the family, their pathetic, shamed life, is his fault.

She is volatile, cruel, disdaining Jeff for his ineptness, his weakness.

She is overwhelming.

Jeff appears beaten, outwardly meek, yet boiling at her open humiliation of him.

I try to intercede, to keep a focus but not knowing at this point even what that is. Joan stalemates me, avoiding my questions and evading my statements. They begin to really battle, assailing one another with details of intimacy, looking to wound, to maim.

The dynamics are explosive and frightening.

Joan is livid, eyes piercing and icy as a rattlesnake's. She declares she will never give her Sean up. Never.

Jeff does not back down.

The tension is held rigidly between them. The room is incendiary.

Then, somehow it ends. There is no resolution. No conclusion, no agreement, no truce. Bob and I leave, thoroughly exhausted and shaken. He had sat and witnessed the unbelievable, stunned. I feel as if I have been inside something dark and dangerous and ugly, something meant to remain hidden.

I am aware that the life of a child is at stake here. A child's life determined by the acts and intentions and emotions of the two people we have just seen. And we have seen but a glimpse.

All the while, Sean waited in his room, listening, having to live in what I am so grateful to be able to walk away from.

That night my sleep is assaulted by the tension and gloom of the visit, of what the full weight of truth must be like for Sean.

The following day Joan suddenly walks into the room. She is visibly trembling, seething with anger. She announces that she has left Jeff and is staying at her mother's, then turns and exits.

It's as if because the game isn't going her way, she won't play.

I look over to see Sean and Terri and Bob stopped in their tracks, mouths gaping, at Joan's display.

For the next several days Sean is reluctant to leave for home on the bus. He looks at me with pitiful, forlorn eyes. Sometimes he tries some old tricks to prolong our time together. I wonder what he is going through, whom he is staying with. I cannot reach Jeff by telephone.

Then I find out that Joan's threat worked. Jeff has given in, apologized, promised not to rock the boat. Joan moved back.

12

Sean's Mastery

Immersed in hate he doesn't have to do anything; he can be paralyzed, and the rigidity of hatred makes a kind of shelter for him.

John Updike

Sean is completely stalemated at home. There is nothing to inspire or support or encourage him to be any other way than he is. He is taken care of but not respected, related to as some kind of problem, something stunted and aberrant. He has so few avenues in which to express himself in a family saturated with guilt and anger and frustration and disappointment and selfishness. His sense of himself must be of someone so apart, so removed, so distanced. He has not been reached; he does not reach out.

I find a blank when I try to sense, to picture Joan and Jeff as being able to step beyond themselves to really connect with Sean, with anyone.

Sean lies around so nonchalant, acting indifferent, bored, yet I know he watches everything. He is quick to follow my slightest direction—"Hey, Sean, come here a minute!"—but it's as if he does not want to act on his own.

I exaggerate his lassitude.

"Perk up!" I suddenly, playfully attack him, pound on his chest, bombarded him with thumps, squeeze his arms and legs and head, cuff his ears, roll him around the floor like a log.

He loves it.

What he adopts at home—what may be necessary for him there—I subvert when Sean is with me. His lethargy is contrived. I break into it. Or I mirror it. My pattern is unpredictable so I can catch him off guard.

Sean is in kind of a dull stupor, waiting for something to happen. I call to him, "Pay attention!", to ensure his alertness, maintain his readiness, enlist his initiative.

He quickly sits upright, anticipatory, looking at me bug-eyed.

"Just checking in," I say. "How's it going?"

I parallel Sean's inertness all morning, acting as if he isn't there just as he acts toward me. Lunchtime approaches and the stakes are raised. He will not give in now after holding out this long. I do not ask, so without any assertion from him he misses eating.

Later, I abruptly invade his aloofness, not in play but searingly direct and immediate. I tell him I want him to be here with me, not gazing away when I look at him, not closing his eyes or covering his ears.

Watching me, he tightly shuts his eyes into a slitted squint.

These acts, these inverted attempts to connect, to relate to me, to reach me by having me reach to him.

I lampoon him, pressing my palms to his closed eyes. He does not like this and pulls my hands down, looking at me somewhat alarmed. I roughly slap on his head and cheeks, really shaking him up.

"That's right, Sean. It's not your game; it's not a game at all. I am here with you. I'm real—you're real."

He looks at me, startled.

I want him to want contact. I want it to be direct and genuine and enjoyable.

Sean's mastery is in displaying the least effort in a given encounter, ensuring that the greater effort will be made by whoever wants him to do something.

Sean's former mastery was in his weirdness.

Spitting and flapping and blowing kept people distant. His infantile cooing and shyness and seeming fragility kept demands of him equally infantile. Above all, his lack of speech and any apparent interest in communicating kept him essentially different, making others question just where to connect with him, if at all.

So now Sean seldom spits or flaps or blows. He carries himself upright and meets my eyes clearly with his own. He nods affirmatively to my questions, complies with my requests. He approximates sounds of "Hi" and "Bye," he signs for eat and drink and toilet and walk and play.

Yet these changes are as much a display of Sean's continued mastery as they are any evidence of learning or progress. I can see how he has changed primarily because it is easier than to resist. By changing he actually decreases the likelihood of my intrusions. And these are very measured and calculated changes, indices of his intellect and awareness.

Something else is happening as well, and whether or not Sean intends it, he is connecting with me. He awaits me, he approaches, he contacts. He expresses himself, giving me his anger and delight, his jealousy and coyness, his fear and pain.

"Hi Sean!"
"Hhunnhh!"
"Hi!"
"Oooloo."
"Hi!"
"Leeeee!"
Bob holds Sean's arms, and I hold his ankles. He whines and twists, watching us, not sure.
"Hi!"
He responds with sounds so close to it, a sea of sounds, then buries a clear, unmistakable "Hi" among them, masking its distinctiveness, disguising his comprehension. He cries without tears as he resists our holds, convincingly upset—then abruptly stops to burst out with a mocking laugh as Bob says "Hi Sean!"

His struggle is tepid theatre.

Sean has spit at me before, bit, pinched, scratched. I have been thoroughly unable to maintain a hold on his sinewy limbs whenever he truly wants to get away.

What began as surprise play quickly degenerates into a pitting of wills. Sean regularly repeats our morning greetings with a plainly enunciated "Hi." Now, as we spotlight him to actually make a choice, he resists. We catch him off guard and he quickly recovers, reverts to what is his arena of power—keeping encounters on his terms.

Inadvertently, something has slipped and I am able to see more deeply into the dark and private space that Sean so desperately and tenaciously wants to control. I stare at him during lunch, I am absorbed in thinking of his power, reflecting how vigilant his maintaining control must be. He flippantly ignores me. Then he looks up, directly at me, wide-eyed, eyebrows arched, a message of "Quit it!" He laughs derisively.

He keeps the strange distance throughout the afternoon, as if toying with me. Suddenly, when the bus arrives, he breaks out crying, watching me as he leaves.

I am trying to come up with a different angle on what to do. I feel Sean is somehow engineering things to confirm his inabilities, to fulfill the expectation that he cannot perform.

We prepare to walk to the library. Both of us are in a good mood. I ask Sean to bring my shoes, which he has done before many times.

Now he pulls a dumb act. He looks at me with fawn eyes and picks up a book. I just return his look. He goes to the shelf for a ball, a pair of scissors, a mirror. I ask again for my shoes. He crosses the room, looking at the shoes, and picks up a chalkboard eraser. I go to him and hold his cheeks tightly, sternly telling him I am not a fool, that I know he knows what he is doing.

He cries. He walks over and brings my shoes.

Loretta and I are sitting together, playing. Sean comes and gently turns my face to him, looking playful. He traces along my eyes, my cheeks, ears, mouth with his fingers delicately, as I have done with him countless times.

All on his own, he shows me this touching humanness.

I believe his is sincerely jealous I was with another child.

We are walking to the library, Bob and Terri and Sean and I, a beautiful clear day in late May. Sean's shoelaces are loose and coming unraveled out of his shoes. His recent trick is to keep his shoes untied. Everyone sees it and ties them for him. Surreptitiously, he later unties them. Cute.

I stop at a bench to have him thread the laces through the eyelets. He starts another dumb act. I do not want to feed into it so I tell him to forget it and we walk on. His shoes start falling off and we keep having to wait for him to slip them back on, only to fall off again after a few steps.

Once more I stop to have him lace the shoes. He toys with me, doing a little, just enough to keep me hooked until he fumbles. The head of a lace almost touching the eyelet only to fall from his fingers. The lace barely through the hole as he reaches to grasp it and it drops again. He laughs mockingly. He has gotten me again. I get up and walk ahead.

Sean stumbles and shuffles along now with his loosened shoes and we ignore it. We finally reach the library and stay at the park awhile. Sean and Terri climb on the wood structures, enjoying themselves. Sean is particularly agile and well balanced, and I have him follow me on the beams and decks and poles.

I tell them we have to leave if we want to get back by lunchtime. Sean has his shoes off, lying on the ground full of sand. He puts them on correctly, then switches then deliberately, looking at me deadpan. I ask him to fix them. He takes them off then back on again the same way.

"No, fix them, come on," I say.

He toys with me some more and I get angry.

"What's the deal, Sean? Why are you doing this?"

He cries.

I console him a bit then say we ought to get back. "Come on, put your shoes on and let's have a nice walk."

He holds the bottom of the shoes to the soles of his stocking feet, looking at me.

"Okay, let's go."

I let him walk in his socks, holding his shoes. I talk with

him as if I have forgotten the whole thing, like it's no big deal. I talk about what we see, the cars, people, the sky. He stops several times to try to put on his shoes, looking anxious now, maybe the game is slipping. I won't let him stop walking.

Back at the room it is time for lunch.

"Hey, you need your shoes on to go eat."

He toys around and I ignore him. He sits with his shoes on the floor, signing for food, looking at me, desperate. It is really pathetic. I sit at the table to read.

He laces his shoes and puts them on correctly, then walks over to me and signs to eat.

I say, "Okay, let's go."

We go to my house and Sean heads straight for the bathroom faucet. I tell him I do not want him playing in the water in the house; we will be going down to the beach soon. Within a minute or so he's flicking and splashing the running water. I reprimand him harshly and he glares at me, then runs around the room very angry, wailing, throwing himself on the floor. He crawls under the bedsheets, covering himself, whining. I tell him to come out, to settle down. He does, pouting.

He stays angry even when we walk to the beach. I have him get in the ocean with me and he makes all kinds of noises, like he is resentful. He looks at me and, as if defiant, splashes me with water. I splash back. He spits a mouthful of water and I spit back. I feel that he is trying to incite my anger more than he is expressing his own. I am just being playful. He does his best to remain tough.

We take a long walk along the beach. I tell him I know he is upset with me but I do not want him to do his water thing at my house. I say that it keeps him away from me and I want to be with him.

He seems to work out of his mood and we walk comfortable and relaxed, checking out crab-holes and seaweed, pointing to clouds and the cruising pelicans.

Back at my house he is still not finished with me. I know he is hungry and he signs for food while turning his head away. I say, "Sean, I look at you when I talk; it's nice to look at someone when you talk to them. I like to see you."

He looks at me, looks away and again signs. I wait to give him some room. I do not want to feed his game. He keeps it up. I tell him that he has to let me know things, that I am not going to pull them from him. He is looking at me.

I begin eating. I do not give him any food. I take out some iced tea and ask if he wants some. Almost reflexively he starts to sign for drink, catches himself, drops his hand.

Just when Sean reveals a new understanding it seems we find a new impasse. It is as if he turns every level of change into a stalemate, a message for me not to expect too much from it.

We have been caught in one of these impasses for several days. When we are at the table with juice and fruit, I ask him what he wants. Sometimes he looks at me and readily signs for drink and eat. Sometimes he looks away, signs, looks back.

Sometimes he pulls his ears.

I want to shake things up a bit and decide to take a long walk to the park, just get out. Soon, Sean is doing his shoe game. His laces are trailing, his shoes fall off and he puts them—of course—on the wrong feet.

"Come on Sean, fix them."

He takes them off and puts them on wrong again. I hold his face between my palms and say I do not want to play these games; I tell him to pick up his shoes and just carry them.

He immediately puts them on correctly. I thank him.

We walk awhile, enjoying the morning. I talk about the warming weather, the clouds, about how I like going places with him. We reach a bench and I ask Sean to sit down so he can lace his shoes. It is an ordeal once more. I get angry. I sternly tell him to lace his shoes. He removes his shirt, wide eyed, innocent. He tries to undo his pants, to take off his socks, all in mock understanding.

He does not touch his laces.

I tell him to get up for us to return, and have him walk back in his stocking feet holding his shirt and shoes. In the room

I say that he has to be dressed before he can eat lunch. He puts his shirt on, then his shoes. On the wrong feet. I walk away.

He approaches me and his shoes are on correctly. He laces them while I talk him through it. He looks at me and signs for food. Lunch is over by this time and all I have is an apple that I give him. He eats it ravenously.

Sean stays in a good mood. He gets the soap bottle and blows some bubbles, holding the wand for me to blow also. We play awhile. Then I sit at the table to write and leave him with the bubble-blowing. I look up and Sean is staring intently at me, studying me. I too pause a moment to consider him. This silent, private, controlled child.

When the day ends, I send a note home with him, asking Jeff to call me. After Sean has left on the bus I wonder how much he knows about our separating for the summer. I think about his recent episodes of defiance and obstinance, and how much they may be his way to shield against his separation. Or, perhaps, even to confirm and assure what he may see as rejection.

I start to pack things from the room into boxes. Sean sits in the stuffed chair watching me, clear, alert. He walks to me from time to time and gives a light touch, or just stands in front of me with an inviting, easy smile. I tousle his hair or squeeze his shoulders, smiling in return, and he goes back to watch me from the chair.

He signs for food and drink at lunch.

I do get a call from Jeff.

He sounds exhausted, spent. He is achingly honest and I feel for him, how wretchedly difficult it is for him to talk with me, expose himself, extend himself. The tension and impotence of his life hover like a terrible succubus.

All of which are echoes of, as they also echo through, Sean.

Jeff again affirms his understanding and agreement with what I am doing. But because of Joan, because of his own fears, his own battered self, because of the years living this way, he cannot offer anything. He gives no excuses. He is resigned, defeated.

I explain that what I am doing may not be worth pursuing in the fall, that something less catalytic and more palatable should be considered. Sean will give them no peace. He is expressing himself, often in anxiety and anger, and Jeff and Joan are only magnifying this with their troubled lives. The contrast of Sean's experience with me and with home will only widen if I continue with him.

As if making a confession, humiliated, in a voice heavy and dead, Jeff tells how Joan forced the issue. She made him choose whose side he is on. Hers, or mine.

We drive to the park at the inlet to spend the day. A sadness hangs over us. Sean is transparent. No games.

We walk through the live oaks with their gnarled and twisted limbs arching overhead. I tell Sean I am going to miss him. I say I am sorry he is living with people who will not reach out. And since he won't either, it must be a strange, bleak standoff.

He takes my arm and puts it around his shoulder, then circles my waist with his arms, firmly, leaning his head into my stomach. I tell him not to give up.

On the night before our last day I have a dream. Bob, Terri, Sean, and I are in some sort of run-down pool hall. We leave and pass a cluster of bushes where there is some frenzied rustling that attracts Sean's attention, and he moves toward it. I am fearful of it being a snake so I hold him back. As I do, a small, pugnacious bird flies from the bushes and attacks Sean viciously on the side of his neck. He panics, terrified, and runs off through the surrounding dense foliage. I chase him. The bird flies off but Sean still runs.

I catch up with him and, still terrified, trembling, he clings to me. He is hysterical. I hold him tightly and console him.

Our final day.

Sean surprises me. He is animated, happy, looking at me direct and sustained and real. He initiates play, contacts me.

We pack up a few remaining things, stopping to play a bit. We walk around the room and he holds me by my waist. He begins a ploy over putting some pillows into a box, but then does it, a sly grin on his face.

He signs to eat. Over lunch I ask if he wants to drink anything and he starts to sign, catches himself, and pulls his ears, deadpan. Then chuckles, grinning, looking playfully at me. I laugh as we finish eating, but I do not give any juice.

Both of us, stubborn to the end.

13

Beyond the Membrane

Truly everything that is really interesting goes on in the dark. One knows nothing of the inner history of people.

Celine

I had been immersed in Sean's life for nine months.

Now, I spend the summer regrouping my personal life. I read voraciously, rejuvenate myself in the sun and ocean. I think about what I have done with Sean, why I did it that way. Where I am going with it.

People hear or ask about what I do so I am often talking about Sean and Terri. About weird kids. Casual conversation shifts into avid yet hesitant curiosity, and I realize just how strangely this territory is viewed. It's as if I live in Siberia or operate a nuclear submarine, so full it is of powerful myths, generating powerful opinions.

But it is even more than that.

The very thought of aberrant children is terribly upsetting, something like cancer, full of mystery, of horror, of something gone frightfully wrong. Something that can be described but not really explained. Something best left to the experts. And pray it doesn't happen to you.

Yet this issue of strange children is still far different.

I talk about Sean and the more I do, the more I find I am

making some sense out of the mystery and the myths.

From the first time I met him, I watched. His compulsive blowing and spitting and flapping could go on for hours. I watched, and saw him as fragile, not comprehending, eerily distant, pathetically incompetent, infantile. And I began to see that what he did was always, somehow, in adjustment to something around him. He was supremely, superbly in touch. He was actually in control of his reality by the patterns and compulsions of being so unusual, so strange, so weird.

It was of no help to say this was organic impairment, or brain damage, or genetic miswiring, or imbalanced biochemistry. No clinical, impersonal, professional jargon, however sophisticated, could offer any help or real understanding into what was going on. It was of no help to present what amounted to an excuse for it. Nor was it of help for Jeff and Joan to sort through the shadowing demons of guilt and responsibility.

It is an infinitely inexact science to describe the workings of a person's biology and physiology at a given point in time, most particularly of the stunning complexities of the brain, of mind and language and perception. It is even more inexact to determine if a particular feature of a person is a cause or is a result of those workings.

So it is not enough to say something is wrong with Sean's brain or genetic map or enzyme uptake. Sean was shaped by the process of his life. If to be used at all, the most fitting application of a medical model would be to recognize the pathology of the entire family system. Clearly these were not healthy, viable relationships between husband and wife, parent and child.

The ways they related and interacted were like a malignancy, and my efforts to examine their lives were painful and severely threatening to them. I act as a virtual poison, bringing air and unshaded light into the dark protected recesses of a morbidly symbiotic, privately anaerobic world.

Sean disturbed people. They become reluctant, awkward,

even afraid to say something to him, to do the wrong thing. Even Jeff and Joan, they keep their distance.

Sean does not speak. That concerned me, but what concerned me more was that he did not attempt to communicate at all, did not seem interested in relating or interacting. He could hear, he could understand, but no one could be sure just when or what he knew. Sean did not speak so he was spoken for and interpreted ("Oh, he doesn't talk . . . He wants . . .") Pampered, patronized, indulged, little was expected from him. In this silent compromise Sean was provided for in exchange for his not interfering, not participating. He was virtually left alone.

Sean's rituals did not really bother me, did not worry me. I had seen and dealt with other far more bizarre and far more tenacious children. Also, I sensed that Sean used these rituals, hiding in them, comforted by them, convincing people there was little else in him. Here is this unfortunate, strange little boy, damaged, pathetic. The best to hope for is to train him to get by.

So this child was strange because he did not speak, he babbled and played with his saliva, did not look at anyone, did not play, this child that seemed so isolated and removed. None of that bothered me.

More than anything else, it was profoundly disturbing to be with a nine-year-old child who showed no curiosity, no interest, no motivation to connect with the world, no spark of being really alive. Sean just did not seem to care about anything, anything at all.

This is what bothered me.

I intruded into his isolate, private compulsions. I disrupted his infantile helplessness. I refused to leave him alone, refused to accept his being compulsive or helpless and he came to give it up.

Yet what he gave up was the only facet of his life that I found him to be actually interested in. Without the compulsions and the infantilism, what remained was a clearer illumination of Sean without all that virtual white noise to get in the way. What was left was this boy who, in glaring obviousness, was not interested in anything in any sustaining, predictable manner.

This Sean that remained, however, was not like some empty, vacant husk of a child, a drone. Sean was even more present, more alert than before, even vigilant, but at the same time supremely aloof and indifferent. Whatever he did—a gesture, a reaction, a compliance—now seemed decidedly calculated, measured.

This further convinced me that his earlier rituals and actions were not from some driven internal need or any fixed condition, but were something functional, if not deliberate. They worked.

More and more frequently Sean was affected by me. I would be relentlessly with him, engaging him, focusing him. I would struggle with an approach, not sure, not clear, I would be methodical and clinical, then spontaneous and serendipitous. Suddenly, Sean would release into laughter, the laughter that joins, eyes sparking, inviting me to share his abandon. Or without warning he would flush with anger, the air hot with it. Or again, he would be caught by surprise, his composure broken. At times, wholly unexpectedly, he would explode with heartbreaking anguish.

I would stumble upon this part of Sean and emphatically, yes, he is affected! Despite how he conceals or controls it. I would know then that if he could be affected, he somehow could be moved. And I kept struggling.

I had been only nine months with Sean to sort through what had taken more than nine years to develop. What happened during those years, including the reasons for Sean's way of dealing with the world, would likely remain hidden and unknowable. Ultimately, unless Sean himself is interested enough to communicate, no one will know exactly what did happen and what in that time did affect him.

I touch Sean's life and I find a thoroughly stolid and somber and implacable and defiant boy on one hand, a raw and anguished and sensitive and unbearably lonely boy on the other, and which is central to his being or which is an outcome of his being remains beyond my understanding.

I touch Sean's life in his family and I touch something diseased, stretched taut and swollen to almost bursting, a meniscal tension that instantly registers my touch, alerted, pained. And like a meniscus, a vital membrane so thin and seemingly insubstantial yet crucial in defining what is inside and what is outside.

I went beyond the membrane.

I entered what is unquestionably the most powerful arena of human life: person-to-person relationship, the singular intimacy of encounter and interaction between people.

Through being with Sean I took access to his family, boldly examining what I could see in what is regarded as especially personal, private, if not sacred. I saw what amounted to mere glimpses into the seamless convoluted web of dynamics that Joan and Sean and Jeff created and recreated continually. Glimpses enough to know I was in volatile territory.

Enough to know there was more going on here than Jeff or Joan would—or could—ever tell me. More than I alone could impact with Sean. Enough to know that what had gone on among these people, what they contain within that desperate membrane, what is expressed through Sean's life, was truly staggering.

It was not at all encouraging.

This family carried a weight, a somberness, a joylessness. Their house held the atmosphere of a morgue. I saw Joan with Sean and she was wrought with tension, tentativeness, facade. Jeff displayed sullenness, barely concealed frustration, diffuse anger. Seeing them both was to see a swirl of embarrassment, blame, resignation, distaste.

Certainly, many of the family dynamics developed as an outcome of their being with Sean. Yet these dynamics just as certainly impacted Sean and who he is as an outcome of his having to deal with his family.

Strictly speaking, Joan and Jeff did not make Sean weird. They did not cause him to be how he is. Not like you hit your thigh and make a bruise, not even like a tree is pruned and tied to make it grow a certain way. It is not at all that deliberate, and not that mechanistic.

Yet they did shape the background for Sean, for his experiences and opportunities; they gave color and flavor and texture and sound and smell, an ambiance, to his life.

I try to visualize Sean being born and raised in this family, the continuing immediacy of it, the unceasing presence, the full reality of it, of being Sean, there.

Of the truth of his life.

I asked Joan and Jeff questions, a lot of questions, probing, often intimate ones. They usually answered me, they tried to answer me, but surprisingly many times they could not because they seemed unable to remember. Over time, what they gave me were pieces of a mosaic from which I attempted to reconstruct a fluid picture. An imperfect process, as all memory is, but especially so without Sean's input. I piece together what Jeff and Joan said on one hand, and look at Sean on the other, and wonder how they fit together.

I ask the question: What do you want me to do?

They reply: Make Sean normal.

14

Reign of Tension

What sets a human being in motion other than life's basic needs? I shook that question hard, and only one thing fell out of it in answer: emotions.

Doris Dorrie

Fetal life is an ocean of sensation.

Carrying her second child, Joan is no longer naive about married life, about parenthood. She and Jeff have juggled the demands of careers, car payments, credit cards, and mortgages against their dreams and the passion of courtship to find that the flair of their marriage seems now more a life of getting by.

When Joan is honest with herself she admits things are not the way they're supposed to be. Admits she is nervous and disappointed about still having to worry about money. Worry about Jeff, his drinking, his temper. She had hoped by this time they would be closer, happier, more secure in their partnership and their future—she can't even think about love—but is afraid to look too closely to see they are not. Again, they are surprised by another pregnancy. As clichéd as it sounds, Joan hopes maybe it will bring them together. Maybe Jeff will take things more responsibly. It hurts her to wonder how long he can hold this job. He seems less of a husband to her, less a father to their son, and more of a figure to them. When he is even around.

Her mother was furious when she found that Joan was pregnant the first time. She was right, that shouldn't be the reason to get married. She has not changed her dislike of Jeff since, nor her blame of him for her daughter's unhappiness. Joan deserved something better. And now this. Another child.

Gradually, increasingly, steadily these sensations register against a background of stress.

Joan is not able to recall the details of giving birth to Sean. Not about how long was her labor, whether she had drugs, about how she felt, how he looked. She remembers the doctors were worried about Sean being jaundiced but nothing came of it. She says Sean cried a lot, was hard to hold.

Joan and Jeff are not able to recall details of Sean's infancy. When he followed things with his eyes. When he sat up alone, crawled, stood up, walked. They could not say when—or if—he babbled, if he imitated sounds. They never wrote things down. He had no baby book. His older brother, their first child, did. Joan and Jeff had a cloak of darkness over what it was like when Sean entered their lives.

It could not have been a life of happiness or enjoyment or pleasure having this new baby around.

They would remember that.

Sean is able to recognize the waves of tension surrounding him. Sometimes they pass to him like jolts of electricity whenever he is touched, touched when he cries or is given food or cleaned or laid in his crib.

This stress is so familiar to him. It is what he knows of the world around him. It is what is real. He keeps a state of readiness, an edgy anticipation, to meet this new world.

Jeff is having another rough day. He hasn't had a good night's sleep for weeks, between the baby up at all hours and having to stay late at work preparing reports. They are pressuring him again and it looks like he will have even more to do now that they cut back and let people go. The car almost broke down again and he still has to fix the air conditioner at home. And he hasn't had any time at all to go out and shoot pictures anymore. Joan really wants out of that house but she doesn't understand that they cannot afford to move now.

Joan struggles to be with her two boys, back and forth, fixing food and answering the phone and getting them to sleep and changing their clothes. She hardly has time to clean up the house a bit—it feels so cluttered—and she'll have to forget about doing laundry for still another day.

She is trying to hold infant Sean and feed the two-year-old, and somehow the mashed peas get knocked all over the floor and wall. Sean is crying and has soiled his diaper.

Jeff comes home to all this and takes Sean to change him while Joan deals with the mess. Sean keeps crying as Jeff gets his diaper off. Sean's cries become screams. He twists and squirms and pulls as Jeff tries to hold him with one hand, wipe him with the other. Feces smear the table, the wall, all over Sean and on Jeff. He talks to console Sean while trying to clean him but the baby keeps twisting and squirming and screaming and the feces are a nasty mess. Sean is worked up hysterically. He screams like only an infant can, gasping and sucking air in his frantic, raw lungs, his little body all tense, his face horribly contorted and reddened. His screams reach deep into Jeff, tearing him up, so worn out with futility and ineptness against this disturbing, intense infant. The room is throbbing with Jeff's sweat and bursting patience when Joan finally comes and picks Sean up in a damp, warm towel, eventually soothing him. Jeff numbly sits down on the sofa.

Any joy at having this new baby has dissipated. He screams for no reason at all, even worse when Joan or Jeff pick him up. He squirms, pulls away. It is an ordeal to change him. Joan can't breastfeed, he is so hard to hold, and she ends up leaving him alone with his bottle.

It is so confusing to figure out his moods, to know what he is going to do, how he will react, to know what he wants, what he likes. Nights are touch and go. Jeff and Joan are never sure Sean will sleep four or five hours or begin crying after only one or two. They are so fatigued. So nervous and frustrated with him. It is all mixed up. What should be good ends up an ordeal. They find it hard to play with Sean, to lie on the floor with him and cuddle, to toss him in the air, to talk baby-talk, to count his toes and blow bubbles on his tummy. So they do not do any of it.

Jeff has no patience. He feels inept, his temper short, so he seldom gets involved. Joan feels uncertain, unsure of herself and what to do, how to handle Sean. He is just too difficult. They are worn out, nerves frayed. And deep down, Joan feels rejected—her baby does not respond to her. It's not supposed to be this way. Deep down, she is hurt and angry. Whatever she tries ends up wrong, she feels rotten, and she finds it easier to just back off.

They let Sean cry it out—he does not want a bottle, does not want a toy, does not like to be picked up, does not need to be changed. They cannot figure him out. It is hard to do, but maybe it is better to just let him cry it out.

Joan's mother takes Sean often. She does not think they are firm enough and anyway, Joan needs a break, and wants to find a job.

Everyone is surprised by Joan's third pregnancy. Her mother and Jeff are upset but Joan insists on going through with it.

The tension is everywhere, is everything.

It is frightening, deafening, painful, relentless.

Sean finds a moment when he feels calm, relaxed. He looks around, shapes, light, shadows, colors. His mother picks him up—that touch again, that sound of her voice. Holds him tight. Sean is a bit nervous, not too sure. He squirms a little. Joan wants him to look at her, wants to see his face, her baby. Holds him out in front of her with her arms. Sean is twisting and rolling and shutting and opening his eyes, unsure, unsettled. Joan has to hold him tighter; talking to him to stay still, she tries to get him to see her by turning his face and body.

That electricity, that sensation. It is coming closer, stronger. Sean whines, squirms. Joan hopes he won't cry, not again, he always cries when she touches him. Please no, not again, she just wants to look at him but he cannot focus on her face, it's a blur, his eyes open and shut, his head turning side to side, and he cries. The calm is gone. Joan is disappointed once more, bewildered, shaken, and puts her crying baby back down.

Over and over, again and again, something goes wrong, does not click. The timing is off. Jeff cannot feel a connection with this baby, not like he could with his other boy. Joan does not want to admit she herself does not yet feel her own attachment to Sean. She worries. She is concerned for Sean, if he is getting what he needs. If she is a good mother. It is so shaky, not knowing, doubting, feeling so awkward, embarrassed, frustrated. Sean seems so distressed around her and she feels it is her fault. Her emotions are in turmoil.

The tension reigns.
Sean's young world is one of stress. He was born of it, lives in it.
He unerringly senses the stirrings of tension. A tentative gesture, a solicitous tone of voice, an awkward touch.
Being with people is like a nerve net. He is instantly connected with their moods and feelings and attitudes. They always want something from him, do this, not do that. It is always intense, so much push, so much anxiety.
An air of anticipation, raised voices, noise, always noise. Disappointment. Anger. Grabbing and pulling, a slap, a spank.
He spends hours alone.
It is quiet and peaceful.
The only place he knows, without the push, without the tension, is his own. It is inside.
It is something he can do.

They cannot get Sean to learn to use the toilet. Every time they try becomes a terrible scene, fighting with him, fighting with one another. It is like he will not even try, will not even sit down. He is always wetting the bed. His clothes are a mess. He just wants to play in the toilet. Jeff gets furious. Joan does not know what to do. Sean is close to six years old and this is just too much.
They cannot handle it any longer. They have Sean stay in

a treatment home for a couple of months. Jeff and Joan feel like they have lost an important battle—they could not get Sean to listen to them—but they had to do something.

In the treatment home Sean quickly learns to use the toilet, and comes back home.

The tension reigns.

They are afraid of Sean, afraid of his remoteness, his unpredictability. Afraid of his will. He seems to have such power, almost cunning. To get him to do anything is always a crisis, an argument, threats and shouts, tempers flying, Sean being grabbed, struck, left in his room. Ugly scenes.

They avoid one another, all living in one house but in separate, parallel lives. They seldom eat meals together. Never go out and do things as a family. It is just too much of an ordeal, embarrassing, always on edge.

They do not have many friends. People seem to look at Joan and Jeff with pity, as if something is wrong with them, too. They cannot feel close with anyone, open up, have fun.

For Jeff and Joan their dismay over Sean is overwhelming. They know something is wrong with him—all the specialists have said it—so this isn't really Sean's fault. He cannot help himself. It is their mutual misfortune. No one is to blame. But then, no one is responsible. It is like living with a kind of alien, this bizarre being that is not part of the usual world. Is somehow outside of it.

Sean cannot connect his moods or feelings with anyone, cannot relate to anyone in ways that do not quicken the tension, pluck the nerve net. If he goes along quietly, keeps out of their way, everything is okay. But soon enough, someone gets exasperated with him.

They do not let him get in the water because he makes such a mess. And frankly, it is so, well, weird. He finds a way though, making a gooey mud puddle and squatting naked in it. Or clogging the toilet so a layer of water covers the floor. And always that blowing and flapping and making strange noises.

He has, unaccountably, become increasingly destructive. Sometimes they find him in such a rage he has torn apart the upholstery or shredded the drapes, like an animal. The more they threaten and yell and punish and spank him, the more they find something else destroyed or sabotaged.

If they leave him alone, the better it is. Especially letting him just stay in his room. He likes it there.

Besides, Joan is busy with the new baby.

15

The Sense of Self

He was wholly at their mercy. If they disliked him he had to be hateful; if they mocked him he became grotesque . . . He was helplessly obedient to the demands of their emotions, reactions, moods.

Ursula LeGuin

I have spent considerable time with children who are severely skewed.

I have tried making connection with them, tried to make sense out of them. I have taken the commonly held view that something was wrong with their mechanics, their brains and nervous systems or genetic blueprints or endocrine functions. I could never get any answers here—true, unequivocal answers—but I learned how to get these children to look and act less skewed. By training them.

I learned, however, that by training a child—which is to have him look and act more normal—I did not get any closer to him, any closer to whatever essence identifies a person.

If I could not discover that essence, I could not reflect it back to him, could not reciprocate our fundamental humanness. And could not convince or demonstrate to the parents that their child was, in fact, a little person worth connecting to within all that weirdness.

Training might make their living somewhat easier. Looking for physiological dysfunction or genetic anomaly might help absolve their guilt. But it did not help me see the child through this: it was only a smoke-screen. It surely never seemed to help the child. He was quite clearly kept at a cool distance, an arm's length study of an afflicted offspring.

I could not shake my suspicion that something else was going on here. Something deeper. Something blacker upon what determines our human condition rather than calling on a dastardly, hidden germ or twisted circuitry. I could not shake my suspicion that this lies squarely in the lap of our baby making and family living, right in the face of how we couple as lovers, as man and wife, as companions, as friends, as parents. Of how we live as social and cultural beings.

It is more than a brain lesion or a hormone secretion, more than an extra chromosome, more than some bad seed. It is beyond any single trauma or accident or episode. These are compelling and enticing explanations, but they are too simplistic, too convenient.

It is blacker to put it into our midst, our person-to-person reality. Into our own dynamics of being human together, of circumstances and attitude and personality and motivation, all complex and convoluted and interconnected. It is confusing, often overwhelming to sort though, volatile to confront, staggering to change.

Which is why it is avoided.

I have seen too many similar patterns to dismiss their significance of these children, of these parents and their children. I see function rather than dysfunction, what works for the child, what makes sense for him.

We are more like one another in sharing a common process of being who we are than we are different by isolating the special characteristics that sort us apart.

If we are programmed at all, particularly in the development of language comprehension, speech, and overall personality, we are programmed in our very sentience. We are predisposed to receive sensations, to be acutely aware of our surroundings, to maintain alertness. From these predispositions arises our primary human feature—interacting with others.

Despite appearances to the contrary, of frailty, incompetence, disability, obliviousness, unresponsiveness, these children are acutely sentient, perceptive, aware. They do not miss a thing.

Their skewed interactions with others are as much a statement about the others as they are about the children—a breakdown in the reciprocating development of what we regard as especially human, of language comprehension, speech, and personality.

The families are featured by something imbalanced, oblique, erratic. Above all, the aberrant child in their midst is strangely seen without being really looked at. Perceived but not given sober, honest, if painful, embrace. The child as alien.

And so the family seems wary, or judgmental, excessively harsh and terse, or indulgently solitious and mawkish. The family unit is not a base of power from which the child can explore and return to and upon which he can develop. In this absence the child's distinctiveness emerges as the power base. As the focal point, the energy sink.

The child emerges, in fact, with a core of self, a solidity. These children maintain an irrepressible will, a determination beyond mere obstinacy or noncompliance to preserve and protect this self, this sense of who they are amidst the howling confusion. They express this self as weirdness, a weirdness we find disturbing to confront, to admit, to understand.

They are a mirror.

They are the canary in the coal mine.

We are disturbed by what we see because deep down it is we, not the children, who have failed to connect.

We live so close to the surface. Available, reactive, expressive. We quickly learn, while so young, that the real world is the one outside our skin. Our private life, truly private and fully alone, eludes us, just beyond reach. We are always so busy, so *on* all the time.

Typically we touch our private lives only in unexpected incidents, of severe grief, illness, crisis, some event that isolates our sense of self, existential, harsh, singular. Usually these are occasions of gravity marked not just by their importance but more because we become acutely in touch with a depth of our very being. A place not mediated by the veneers of role playing, of the consensus reality we accept and abandon to. Not answering to anyone, not adjusting to anyone.

We well may give up a certain sense of self, a certain knowing of our own being, by living close to the surface. Which may be why we are often unprepared to cope with the elevator drop sensation that occurs in a crisis, forcing us suddenly to our singular, interior identity, deep down, far from the surface.

Sean has not partaken of life on the surface. Which partly explains why he is so different, so disturbing; his life derives from the other extreme. His life, his sense of who he is, of being alive, resides deep, frighteningly deep.

There, he is more than alone, down to where he is solid, to where only he is, so far down that no one can touch him.

The truth of his life.

I dropped down to where Sean is. I met him at a place each of us knows, no matter how we may fear or deny or avoid or protect it. If nowhere else, there we are alike.

Aloneness. Utter aloneness.

I was absorbed with Sean, with discovering the truth of him.

As concerned, distraught parents, as intelligent adults, Joan and Jeff earnestly solicited my help. I assumed, in full naiveté that they would be sincere allies in my efforts to make their relationship with Sean a healthy one.

I came to realize that despite their stated intentions and their intelligence, they were as dependent upon Sean's weirdness as he was. They did and said things that were more inhibiting and restrictive of growth than to encourage and nurture it. They were prone to anxiousness and confusion and tension and conflict, in their body language and mannerisms, what they talked about and how they expressed it, in what I could put together of their personalities and emotions.

I saw these patterns of Jeff and Joan as corollaries to patterns Sean used and grounded himself with. What Sean did and what he did not do was the central element of their lives, as it had been for quite some time. The significance of this element, this theme, this issue grew and evolved over the years in intensity and proportion, and what Jeff and Joan did and did not do may well have served to amplify the theme itself.

Sean's weirdness encouraged distance.

Joan and Jeff's distance nourished Sean's weirdness.

By focusing primarily on and by always viewing through Sean's weirdness, it not only remains but is given life and actually becomes validated. And Sean is not reached.

Whatever sense of self Sean derives from his parents is through this focus, and the self that is affirmed and defined through them is far from being positive and viable.

Just as I needed to intrude and seduce and scheme to leverage change with Sean, I would similarly have to do with Jeff and Joan if they were to help in any substantial way. I could not simply rely upon their reasoning abilities or appeal to their hearts.

My expectations for both Sean and for his parents were admittedly high, perhaps entirely unrealistic.

I could empathize with Joan and Jeff in their eroding, disappointing, even tragic lives. I felt deep empathy for Sean, fragile, sensitive, unfit for the world. I often pitied them, each member of this fractured family. My presence for all of these people was a source of uneasiness and worry and resentment and even pain. At times I thought it would be best for me to just back off, pull away, leave their roles intact.

But I would not pull away.

As adults, Jeff and Joan could ultimately determine their own lives; they had resources and abilities. I could leave them alone. Except, they were not just determining their own lives but those of their children, Sean in particular. And the life they fostered for him was not a healthy one.

Sean clearly showed me that there was a great deal more to him. He responded to me and to the world in an entirely unexpected way. I would not back away now. I would continue to intrude on their lives, to be absorbed with Sean. I would continue to push.

Because there was one more thing. Sean was a living clock; puberty was fast approaching. I had to act if I was to have any appreciable impact on empowering his life. The scale of biological, neurological, emotional, and social factors will escalate and compound tremendously once he hits puberty, and likely will put him well beyond my or anyone's ability to help. Whatever I could do had to be put in place now.

The truth of Sean's life remains hidden behind questioning of Joan and Jeff, and will never be known without their full willingness to disclose emotionally and psychologically charged memories.

Yet even at that, there is a uniqueness of the mind and perception of a child that is entirely apart from that of an adult. The full reality of a child, the significance of events, quite likely is not even approached by the adult version.

The adults, the parents, Jeff and Joan see the child, Sean, a child living on a temperamental fringe. A severely distant child, preoccupied with bizarre routines. Does not speak. Does not seem to care, to have any feelings. Without a child's curiosity or sense of play.

Their lives as parents, as adults, as man and wife, have been a plodding ordeal, a fog, a bad dream if not an outright nightmare. Without clarity, without scope, without direction. Their relationship with one another is all blurred.

Sean, on the other hand, has been living inside a fluid, a nerve net, intensely aware, instantly connected. His sense of who he is has developed more out of self-preservation and self-reliance than from attachments, from relationships that have been in an ocean of tension, awkwardness, ambiguity. Caught within the taut web of failure and pathology and inability and incompetence anticipated by his parents, Sean avoids what is new, different, unknown, unexpected. He takes no chances. He rigidly maintains his closed routines, maintains a reality not reliant on trust or attachment. Indeed, what he knows of attachment, of connection, is predicated by anxiety. What Joan and Jeff see as a distant child is evidence of the proportion of this anxious attachment. Sean's distance and the anxiousness of attachment have not allowed the development of an empathic perspective. Not only do Joan and Jeff not know this boy, this child, their son, they in fact fear him. Sean has not been able to model the world from other points of view, to adopt reality through the eyes of his mother and father, leaving him further within his egocentric and idiosyncratic world.

Without a viable, reciprocating, non-threatening, dependable relationship with another person, Sean cannot learn trust, empathy, exchange. There is no basis for curiosity, initiative, motivation.

Without a relationship, it is hard to conceive of any way Sean could have either the desire to occasion to learn to speak. His thorough comprehension of language is a result of and evidence of his alertness and intellect, of his well-developed ability to get by. However, without an important involvement with someone from early onward, without the seemingly innocuous play of vocalizations and exchanging of sounds in a context of trust and security and pleasure and constancy, there is no reason to speak or communicate. Only to understand, privately, what was going on.

The truth of Sean's life remains hidden within his strangeness, left for me to interpret.

In Sean's infancy, Jeff and Joan were incapable of understanding needs, unable to correctly read them, satisfy them. Sean never learned to expect others to gratify what he wanted. His parents felt bad, unsure, tentative, incomplete, frustrated. It was a short step to turn some of these feelings to the apparent cause of them, to Sean, in anger and rejection and punishment.

Sean remained unable to communicate his own feelings to insensitive parents. Insensitive not because they did not care, but because they had developed a picture of their son where he had no feelings—or if he did, they were feelings so strange or out of reach that Joan and Jeff had stopped trying to understand them.

Sean emerges as the power base.

His own alienation gave him focus, grounded him within the anxious, assaulting nerve net. His alienation gave Jeff and Joan focus, grounding them, occupying them, defining them. Without which they would then have to squarely face what else their own lives were, what else their live gave them.

Sean with Jeff and Joan, Jeff and Joan with Sean, shuffling and sending and reading distorted emotional messages. An ocean of disorganized, confused, ambivalent patterns.

And Sean, swimming in that ocean.

16

Back Together

He found that he was capable of desiring things outside his life.

Mary LaChapelle

The summer ends.

Sean arrives as a facsimile of himself of a year ago, jacket pulled over his head, cooing, squeezing his eyes shut and grinning moronically. He surveys the situation and finds not only is he no longer the focal center—he is off the hook!—but sees the entertainment value of the virtual circus around him. Not having to perform, by action or evasion, he just stays aloof.

The day comes to a close and as bus time approaches Sean suddenly becomes genuinely and greatly upset. He whines, coming to me, wanting my attention while I am busy orchestrating with the new kids. I console him as best I can. He seems truly disturbed at having to leave, to return home, as if he wasted the day away acting cool. He looks continually to me in appeal as he boards the bus.

The arrangement is quite different now. I had to take on four other boys, each intensely demanding in his own constellation of weirdness, each fully containing his own elaborate history. Terri went on into a more regular classroom; he will make out okay. Bob moved to another city where he will have his own program. I know I will really miss him.

I share the charge of this with Sandi and our two assistants. So I have to deal with Lou and Nick and Billy and Philip, with their families, figure out who they are and where to go with them. I have to enlist Sandi and Sue and Marilyn in this amorphous, spontaneous, intuitive process, unlike anything they have ever seen, of working daily with these children. On top of all this I decide to carry Sean. There is no place else for him to go that would not entirely lose him.

I do not want to lose him. I will carry him because I know his only chance is to get away from his family. I will carry him because I feel I am his only connection. His only chance.

Sean is thoroughly amused.

He watches me do with these boys what I did with him. Watches me direct Sandi and Sue and Marilyn. He stays on the periphery, as the demands of the new kids are intense and constant and fully engaging for me, but he stays alert.

I am surprised and relieved at how present Sean actually is. I had anticipated many scenarios of how he would return from a summer at home, wondering how much I would have to start over with.

But he is alert, he is available when I want him, he is responsive. He knows the basics of the routine, to be there, to pay attention, and he knows the effect of holding out. For the most part he wants to be there—or does not want to deal with what happens if he acts like he is not. He paints, does puzzles, looks at magazines with Sue. He signs for eat and drink and toilet and walk. He comes to me periodically, for affection, for play, for just being near.

I have a strong sense of specialness of him, more than mere fondness or familiarly, the feeling of a bonding.

Yes, a bonding.

I know I cannot go much further with Sean as long as the gridlock exists. His emotional life is at its limits, having to contend day upon day with the ambiance of tensions and vacancy of his home. As a victim. A scapegoat. An antagonist.

My time with Sean has taken a profound shift. I feel I only

want to affirm our bond, to strengthen my belief in him, to broaden his belief in himself. I no longer need to explore or prove his capabilities as much as I want to catalyze his motivation.

I know what he can do. I want him to want to do it.

So, often he simply just hangs out. He enjoys the benefits of his graduate position. He is delightful to be around. A bemused observer, frequently a jealous intruder, at times a sincere assistant. At any rate, he has certainly outgrown this format.

He does not need to be brought out. He is here.

Suddenly, I plunge into an episode that reminds me of how his emotional life is so suppressed.

I am busy with the other boys and today Sean is not content with just watching. All morning he pulls his socks and shoes thing, shoes on the wrong feet, socks on his hands.

I tell him he doesn't have to do this. It won't get him any more time with me.

I have him sit out, and say he cannot do anything else until he puts his shoes and socks on.

He pees in his pants.

The bell sounds for lunch. He still has to sit.

Back and forth, testing, testing, pushing, trying to trap one of us. One shoe on the wrong foot. Shoes on without socks.

Just as the bus arrives he defecates in his clothes, looking defiant.

Sighing, I apologize to him that even this still will not work, and I send him on. I make sure, for all it may be worth, to say I care for him. I watch the bus until it turns out of sight from the driveway.

Jeff and Joan will not see me together. Their summer must have been difficult.

I talk with Jeff on the telephone and he sounds utterly spiritless, used up.

When Joan comes by one afternoon, all facade is dropped and her message is clear. I have permission to find a place for Sean.

I continually remind myself what a powerful statement Sean is making. He prefers to be with people. He stays around me most often but readily goes to Sandi and Sue on his own or when they ask. I remind myself that a year ago this was a boy who had little or nothing to do with anyone, preferring his strange compulsions. I remind myself of the days and months of struggling to find a way in, cat-and-mouse, the endless battles of wills, the shifts of power.

Now, Sean is so steady.

Each day connects to the next, as it is connected to the day before. We can build on the subtle agreements and understandings that give continuity to a relationship, the intimate collection of touches and glimpses and gestures and feelings that allow a person to know another.

He is a wonderful and most special boy to be with. He is at ease with himself and extends this ease with others. Around people he no longer stands out but looks like—and is regarded as—just a quiet kid.

Usually one of us has Sean join in something we are doing with another of the boys. While Sue tries to get Nick to finger-paint, Sean will put on a smock, get a sheet of paper, wet it, and then smear it with colors, keeping a sober, almost professional face. See Nick, like this.

I ask Lou to put his jacket on the coat-hook and he escalates into a frenzy of gnashing teeth and gut-wrenching screams and epileptic-like thrashings. While I deal with this, Sean sits, watching. Then, eyes sparkling, he laughs directly at Lou, walks to him and pulls Lou's shirt from his pants which drives Lou into a renewed series of howls and contortions. I cannot help smiling at Sean's clear impishness.

Sandi sits with Philip for him to imitate her putting various wood shapes into corresponding openings in a box. Philip is oblivious. Sean watches. Sandi takes Philip's hand, places it on a piece, guides it to the hole. All Philip has to do is let go. "Okay Phil, that's it. Drop it."

Nothing.

Sean reaches over, takes the piece from Philip's still outstretched hand, and puts it in the box. Expressionless.

We find ourselves truly enjoying Sean being around. I spend time alone with him whenever I can. Sometimes to sit under the trees, blowing soap bubbles, sharing the silence or talking to him, sometimes to wrestle in the grass. We relax together on the large floor pillows and look through illustrated books of animals or exotic places or impressionist paintings.

More and more I give him things to do, puzzles and complicated matchings and sortings. Without any issue he now imitates the sequences and arrangements with the Cuisenaire rods. Sean has a quick eye for pattern recognition, so I want to do more with it.

I play around with letter matching, with initial word sounds and their relevant objects, with pictures of things associated with their real objects, with objects associated with other objects. Probing the edges of language.

Sean is comfortable with his signs and we start new ones. We casually sit together on the rug and look through the sign book, trying different ones. No pressure.

Each week Sean spends a couple of hours with the speech specialist. She runs through the standard exercises for plosives and glottal stops and fricatives and aspirates. Sean is somberly compliant but never beyond the directions, never any spark of his own doing. My suspicion is that this arrangement is too contrived for him and he is not that comfortable with a total stranger.

Through all this, Sean is actually using his voice quite regularly. We say "Hi" or "Hello" and he pushes out a breathy "Hhaah!" or "Hhuuh!", and to our goodbye is his quick, precise "Buh!" He repeats our names with a single blast of the initial sound. But for any self-initiated expression he always uses sign.

The music specialist comes in often and we do a lot of improvising, mainly to just get the boys to make vocal sounds. We sit around in a circle and chant nonsense syllables or choruses of vowels. Sean usually joins in without any prompting.

A favorite is the can band. Everyone has a tin can or two of various sizes and a pair of wooden sticks. We find all kinds of rhythms, singing along, and if it doesn't exactly sound like music it does feel pretty good.

I have Sean go to a physical education class once or twice

a week. I tell him it is time for gym and he walks through the halls and out to the field by himself, while I watch surreptitiously from a window. He really has no interest in activities and games, particularly, but he goes willingly. He stands around, bored, not at all following the system of movements and instructions that are part of kickball and baseball and basketball. Sean agreeably enough does what the coach tells him (throw the ball, run over there) but without any enthusiasm or continuity. So, although Sean is far from a team player, the other kids tolerate him, and in his own way he is part of something that was inconceivable a year ago.

The coach has regular drills and Sean dutifully waits in line, takes his turn. Soon the coach finds that Sean is rather skilled at keeping a ball at his feet while running, soccer style. Once he is fed the ball, he stays very focused and will run forever with it. Now the coach has something to really work with and Sean is fit into some modified games. He actually seems to like it.

So Sean goes through the day very agreeably, involved, relaxed, expressive, social.

But I am troubled by one thing that he does more and more frequently, and I think it is a direct message of his confusion. Almost every day now he wets his pants. Sometimes two or three times. And when he does, he looks genuinely scared as well as apologetic. Not with the defiance and deliberateness of before. I don't make anything of it other than have him clean up and change, and I reassure him.

And I feel privately terrible for him. It is as if he's a frightened puppy, expecting to get scolded.

And put out of the house.

17

Far from Home

Aloneness is our only birthright. With any determination we can turn aloneness into independence—but nobody guaranteed us love.

Erica Jong

My search for a place for Sean is not very fruitful. After reviewing the group-home situations I quickly reject them as options at all. Similarly out of the question is a nearby private residential center, and the same with the state-run institutional homes which, of course, are not anything close to a home. My visits and calls to these facilities are harsh reminders of how utterly dehumanizing is the labeling, warehousing, and drugging of scores of children, adolescents, and adults, victims of a failing social fabric.

I put my efforts into soliciting and screening for foster or adoptive homes. Again a bleak picture. Most of the prospective people are eliminated after a phone call or two, the rest after a simple visit. Finding another home, that is, another family, willing to embrace a child not their own is rare enough. Finding one truly willing and capable of embracing a child as different as Sean will be nothing short of miraculous. The visits I make after a seemingly promising conversation reveal a family that is well intentioned but more endeared to a certain idea or stereotype of what Sean should be like than who is he really is.

So we carry Sean.

He continues to remain remarkably steady. He continues to

wet his pants.

I am running out of prospects, beginning to lose hope.

I bring a video camera and film the boys, film Sandi and Sue and Marilyn, film the parents. We play back sequences on the monitor for review and critique , or just for entertainment. It is an extremely powerful device for self-examination; equally powerful to reveal patterns of dynamics in how the boys relate with us, in how they and their parents interact. The camera often captures what the eye or the mind does not. And the playback is hard reality. Inarguable.

We film Sean mostly for its own sake, not needing the critique as with the other boys. His reaction to viewing himself is a very even curiosity. He readily points himself out when asked and recognizes all the others. He is quite amused at seeing the histrionic vignettes of the boys we frequently record.

After several conversations with a prospective adoptive family on the telephone and in person, I arrange for them to visit the room. Sean has been used to visitors as I regularly have people come for various reasons, professionals, friends, specialists, students, administrators. I usually tell him simply that someone is coming and then introduce them to one another by name, giving no title or explanation of why they are there, other than to just visit. Apart from returning a handshake, Sean accepts their presence without obvious regard.

But with this couple Sean is different. I instructed them earlier to merely observe, to be responsive and polite if approached but not to initiate conversation or contact with any of the boys.

Sean is agitated and does not stay by himself as I ask while we are otherwise busy with Lou, Philip, Nick, and Billy. He comes to be near me. I let him. We do some puzzles and things together, paint with the other boys, but I know I am putting on a show in a way and I am sure Sean knows it, knows he is part of the show. The main character. But he still handles it well, very well actually, with all the awkwardness and pressure he must sense.

We all eat lunch together and everyone tries to be casual and natural, but I feel it is much too obvious. After the couple leaves I take Sean alone and tell him what it was about. And I apologize. I tell him, and I mean it, that I will not do that again. If someone is visiting to check him out I will say so.

The couple does not answer my calls for almost two weeks. I finally reach the young man and he embarrassingly says they cannot do it, they are sorry, but it is not for them.

Sean has been wetting his bed at home.

With us he does so well, acting almost like an assistant, as well as a capable, attentive student. It is as if the more we clearly regard him with respect the more he demonstrates his equalness to the task, displays a smoothness of character.

Then again, I am seeing something else that is disturbing. As Sean becomes more at ease with Sandi and Sue, and reciprocally the more at ease they are with him, Sean allows more intimate play. In their sessions Sean is infantile, passively accepting and enjoying their touch and caressing, but even beyond that. He lies close to them, curled up, fetal, eyes closed, fists clenched. Sometimes he comes up with a piece of plastic in his hand that he holds to his mouth and presses saliva on with his tongue.

He does not do this with me. Perhaps because I am male, perhaps because I am more familiar somehow. Sandi and Sue can be maternal with Sean, something I can never be. And he only acts this way with Sue or Sandi, not Marilyn; she is still scared of him.

We have a Thanksgiving picnic and invite the families. Everyone is to bring something. We spread blankets under the trees on the playground and set out all the food. It's a real show. The boys are clearly confused about how they should act between us and their families. The families are awkward at the informality. Boys and families are unsure of what is expected of them. Which is nothing more, of course, than simply to be themselves. Which is precisely what is confusing to them.

Joan does not come, the only mother that doesn't. She sends in a nice casserole on the bus with Sean.

Prospects for a place for Sean dwindle. Christmas approaches, a poor time for these kinds of changes.

I hear of a possibility and make another, now routine, telephone contact. After a few more conversations they seem sincere in wanting to meet Sean.

I decide to visit them at their home and make the scenic drive with Sean one pleasant morning. I have already told him what this is about, and I talk some more to reassure him, to explain exactly what we are doing.

Stuart and Mary have a quaint, charming home in a wooded neighborhood. They are a young, personable couple, intelligent, sensitive, warm. Mary quickly takes to Sean and surprisingly he is amenable. She is not at all patronizing and addresses him respectfully as a ten-year-old boy. They go to tour the house and I talk with Stuart.

He and Mary are childless and, after numerous confirmations of their infertility by specialists, came to the decision to adopt. They are active with children in church groups and eventually want to take in several to live with them. From what I have told them, they are very much intrigued by Sean.

Mary and Sean return. Very naturally Stuart begins talking to him and soon they go off together. Again I note the respectful rapport Stuart conveys. Mary confirms what I also found in Stuart to be a level-headed realism in the consideration of adopting Sean. She admits she is unsure of him but not at all afraid. She really likes him.

We find Stuart showing Sean their piano, which he plucks with disinterest. I sense his self-consciousness. Now is a good time for us to leave Mary and Stuart alone, so I ask Sean to take a walk with me.

There is a lake at the end of their street and we drink some juice, sitting on a bench, looking at the glassline surface of the water encircled by the skeletal elegance of pond cypress. Like a Japanese painting. Sean seems relaxed. I ask him to look at me and he does. I say I think they are pretty nice people and I like them. I want him to feel comfortable in letting me know what he thinks, how he's feeling. Sean alternately watches me and then his juice carton, sucking at it through the straw. I ask him if he's okay.

This checking with him, how he is, how he feels, what's up. It has evolved from the days of my expecting him to pay attention, to be alert, responsive, present, the days of expecting the most basic expression of agreement or disagreement, desire or refusal, affirmation or negation. Yes, or no. From the days of being nothing more than rote imitation, a nod of the head or a shake from side to side, it has developed into a genuine, almost endearing form of communication between us. Sean has learned to express himself in a way that is clearly relevant but also something more. With a personal flair, a style.

He is quick to let me know his refusal as a demonstrative, emphatic, abrupt turning of his head. No. At other times he confirms he is okay, that things are fine, with a certain look, an eye contact held just long enough to be neither forced nor furtive. But more often, along with the look, he gives a nod. A deliberate, stylish nod, vintage James Dean. No question.

Now, while he is sucking at his straw, I ask him what he thinks.

He looks up, holds it an instant, and nods.

Several days later we arrange for Stuart and Mary to visit the room. Of course this time it is all aboveboard, and when Sean is greeted he returns handshakes and hugs with naturalness, even a bit of enthusiasm. He remains at ease throughout the day, perhaps showing off a little, and I wonder if he is really trying to win them over.

Which he does.

Mary and Stuart continue to visit regularly, informally. They take Sean to lunch with them. They stay around with us through the day and paint and sculpt clay and sit in with the can band. I meet often with them and discuss all the possible scenarios to consider. I do not want there to be any illusions, and as best as I can anticipate, no surprises. We begin the paperwork for Sean to be legally adopted.

They want him.

I have made sure Joan and Jeff know what I am doing and I telephone them every week or so. Now it is time to meet with them in person, and one evening I go to their home.

A lot has happened since my last visit here, yet the atmosphere is still funereal, staid, frozen in time. The pretenses of socializing are minimized, no small talk is made. Sean is in his room while I sit with Jeff and Joan and describe to them the recent events with Stuart and Mary. To my surprise Jeff has turned the television off.

Joan is quite moved, likely by the reality of facing something that has been hovering for so long as such a loaded issue. She asks questions about their personalities, their character, about their home and their capability for providing a living. It is understood that neither couple will, nor should, meet the other. And when it does occur, the transfer will be final. There will be no visits. Stuart and Mary will be fully Sean's family.

The impact of this, I see, is difficult to bear. Jeff and Joan have known this would be the case ever since they decided to go through with it, but it is difficult nonetheless. There are no tears, no trembling faces, no quivering voices, yet the air is clearly, palpably charged with emotion.

Jeff has been exceptionally quiet the entire evening, quiet but attentive, even scrutinizing. He now speaks, addressing Joan directly.

He says it is time.

They exchange looks, sustained and deep. Now it is Joan who is weak and fearful, leaning to Jeff who is now strong, resolved. In this crisis they are together, a couple.

I wait for them to break the mood. For a while I am not present as they exchange looks and feelings, contemplate the depth and breadth of what they are doing.

Then the spell is loosened. Joan asks if I want to say goodnight to Sean. I knock on his door and enter—thinking suddenly that no one has likely ever knocked on his door to enter— and he is lying on the floor playing with stuffed animals. He looks every bit as much as any kid in his room, playing with stuffed animals as imaginary friends, heroes, villains. He smiles at me and gets up, and we exchange the gentle affections that I realize have become so natural and spontaneous with us, but so scarce and awkward here in his home.

As if just remembering, Joan opens his closet while telling me of the hole she and Jeff had recently found there where Sean had dug under the floor. I listen somewhat absently and she talks as she always has about Sean, as if he isn't there—but even more insultingly, as though he can't understand.

There, in the corner, is a fist-sized hole. Joan describes in partial amusement, partial ridicule, partial disbelief, how they found this hole that Sean must have had for years. She reaches down and shows me the pieces of fur, the scraps of soft cloth, the assortment of plastic and cellophane, a pair of slippers that had disappeared long ago. Then it hits me. I picture Sean furtively huddled in the closet with his secret soft things, that he actually somehow dug this hole in the floor, that he had this place for years.

I watch Sean's face as Joan talks and he is trying to stay collected and impassive and I am about to burst, this brash violation of his private meaning, the utter poignancy of his need to have it, to hide it, the sheer insensitivity of his mother.

I look at Joan and she is still rattling on, insensitive now as ever, patronizing, belittling, and I know she does not deserve Sean's true reaction. Nor mine.

I drive home under a vast mute darkness and ache to cry for him.

Things are in gear.

The paperwork is being processed and, pending the necessary clearances, a date is scheduled. Sean will attend the local school and the teacher is very receptive to working with him. Stuart's and Mary's excitement builds. They prepare a room in their house for Sean, painting and furnishing it tastefully. One or the other visits Sean during each week.

He is right there, meeting this thing head-on. It is almost surreal to me that this is taking place.

The final step is contingent upon Stuart and Mary

completing some technicalities, and they are to contact me when everything is ready.

A week passes without word. I cannot reach them by phone. At the end of the following week I get a message to call Stuart.

I am thoroughly stunned.

The impossible has happened.

Unknown to me, Mary had been feeling strange the past few weeks which she and Stuart attributed, naturally, to the anticipation and anxiety of preparing for Sean. Her symptoms continued, troubling them, and she went to her doctor.

He congratulated her on her pregnancy.

Stuart is sincerely and profusely apologetic, knowing how virtually worthless it is to say so, how irreparable.

18

Cunning, Intellect, and Will

The boy felt a sense of liberation of failing the first test, a sense of freedom that went with not living up to what someone expected of you so that they never again would have to expect anything of you, which would allow you the freedom to live up to what they no longer expected of you.

Thomas Glynn

Without proper measures of Sean's real intelligence as determined by psychometric testing, he will remain restricted in any social and educational opportunities. But in large part the social and educational experiences are necessary in order to learn the kinds of skills and tasks the tests use to measure intelligence.

Caught, fettered. A neat, circular trap.

If I could not change the reality of Sean's home life, perhaps I could improve his chances of getting better school opportunities. I step up the pace of focused work with Sean. What have been more or less games and pastimes now take on more meaning and scrutiny. I develop work derived from the concepts to be used in the testing. I give Sean increasingly demanding arrangements to show that he can discriminate, associate, categorize, and imitate. Above all, I want to get Sean used to the process of performing, doing something someone else wants him to do. Because he still, regularly, stalemates.

After a few weeks I think it is time to try so I have Gary, the psychologist, come in. Sean has already met him several times, mainly observing in the room. Gary readily agrees with me that Sean's social reluctance and lack of speech seriously mask his intelligence. Gary uses a particular series of tests that do not need any kind of verbal response or answer, but instead require some demonstration of a understanding of the question.

He begins by asking Sean to complete some simple imitation of block patterns. Sean looks at me, like what's up here. I had told him earlier that Gary wants him to do some things, but now Sean is clearly very guarded.

He looks at Gary, at me again, then completes the pattern. Okay, no big deal. Gary sets up more tasks and they become increasingly more complex. I sense it is not going to fly.

Sean is given a wooden tile with a pattern of colored shapes on it.

On the table sits a box that has similar patterns across its face with corresponding slots. Sean is asked to drop the tile into the matching slot.

He doesn't look up. And puts the tile in an incorrect slot.

On a hunch, Gary hands it back to Sean, saying nothing. He drops it into another incorrect slot. Gary again gives it back. Sean takes it. His hand almost reflexively extends directly to the correct slot then suddenly drops it in another one. This is so obvious, Gary and I exchange glances. Sean is deadpan.

Gary continues to repeat the same sequence. Each time Sean drops the tile incorrectly until he has used every slot except the correct one. Gary then hands Sean each of the remaining tiles one at a time. Sean appears to drop them into the slots entirely at random but not once in a correct match.

As many times before, when I try to catch him off guard with my own hidden agenda, Sean quickly reads through it and decisively, purposefully retreats. Or sabotages.

And just as many times, I have found this approach to be somewhat distasteful in its deceit. Then I end up leveling with him, simply respecting him with the truth.

Which I do now.

I am convinced of the importance of these sessions I arrange for Sean to practice. And I expect Sean to agree with their importance. I tell him why, what they are for. The sessions become sober events, a daily routine of seriousness.

Sean indulges me awhile.

Then he stalemates.

I get angry, frustrated. I know he can do these things.

He knows I know.

I am asking him to match dot patterns. He picks up the correctly matching card, an instant of eye contact, puts it down and picks another card. Looking at me he places it deliberately on the panel.

I glare at him, saying nothing.

He averts his eyes.

I drill holes in him with my stare.

He squirms uncomfortably. He reaches over and removes the unmatching card to the pile. Again, with a flashing glance to me, he picks the correct one and puts it back down.

His hand wavers over the pile of cards. He selects another unmatching one.

I immediately lurch across the table and shove him in the chest with my open hand, backward in his chair and onto the floor in a crash. He scrambles to his feet, thoroughly shocked.

I leave the table and go sit on the carpet area facing the window to stare outside at the trees, the sky, completely engulfed in my fury. I have no idea how much time passes when I realize Sean has come over and is sitting next to me. I stay wrestling with my clouded thoughts, still heated and righteous.

I look at him. He is calm, focused, very present. Looking right at me. With vehemence I unload on him, scolding, lecturing, browbeating, pontificating. I get lost in the flood of my own arguments.

Hesitantly, Sean extends his hand and gently touches my face.

I falter a bit.

He then frames my face lightly between his two hands. I stop talking.

Sean delicately traces my mouth, my nose, cheeks, the corners of my eyes. I soften, hold my hands out, palms up, and he grasps them. We look directly into each other's eyes. The arguments that were so lucid and certain and vitriolic now become limp and embarrassing. I try to explain myself to him.

He places a soft and cautious hand to my lips, looking at me.

I feel ungrounded, muttering to myself as Sean watches steadily, compassionately. My dependence clearly is on words to work myself out of this, yet it seems so insufficient, irrelevant. It is as if Sean is revealing a secret. Look how much more is available if you didn't rely so much on words.

With nothing left to say I reach to him and we embrace. Holding, silently absorbing one another's warmth, strength, affinity.

I realize Sean is softly crying, his tears wet on my shirt. Then we part. Sean rises, taking my hand, and leads me to the table. He straightens his chair and sits, completing the matching arrangement without a moment of hesitation.

Gary is with Sean for the formal testing. I am watching from the side, away from them. They run through a series of basic skills and Sean is all business, focused, competent. Gary presents the more advanced tests. Sean balks a moment, then quickly, methodically completes them. He has not looked up. He covers his face with his hands and cries quietly.

Gary says they are finished. I look at Sean and say thank you. He uncovers his face and rapidly scrambles the testing materials on the table, then gets up and throws himself onto the beanbag chair.

The testing results conclude it is no longer appropriate to consider Sean as retarded. He is now eligible for more normalized schooling.

19

Accepted

If your parents disapprove of you and are cunning with their disapproval, there will never come a new dawn when you can become convinced of your own value. There is no fixing a damaged childhood. The best you can hope for is to make the sucker float.

Pat Conroy

Sean remains the star of the room. He relates on a genuine, human level. What was formerly his greatest deficit and what kept people from him has developed into a marked attribute. He seeks people out and, remarkably, they now enjoy him.

Yet he still holds back. He is not fully free, spontaneous, curious, not in the ways of a child. I see this, Sean's absence of childlike, unrestrained motivation, as an echo of his family's stasis.

They have not moved from their sullen, defeated, rigid posturing with him. The gloomy resignation that pervades their attitudes negates any sense of change, of incentive, of initiative. In the stormy power plays that define their family life, the low profile is the best course, outlined with irregular bursts of emotional warpage, truly ripe conditions for their network of passive-aggressive interactions.

Sean continues to shuttle between worlds, one where his assertiveness is welcomed and encouraged, the other where his virtual anonymity is preferred. No matter how positively and dramatically Sean has opened, risking trust, he cannot begin to integrate this openness so long as he is subject to the repressiveness and defeatism of his home.

On an impulse I telephone Archie.

I have known him now for some seven or eight years, keeping contact on that rare and special basis that blends the professional with the personal, the mutual respect and affinity that characterizes it. Archie and a handful of his colleagues are directors of their own residential school which they started several years ago after becoming disgruntled with the public education system.

Their program is stunningly impressive.

The students range in age from eight to eighteen, from all manner of backgrounds and circumstances. There is a full span of curriculum, from the traditionals of math, sciences, language, and literature, to the humanities, social sciences, current events, and beyond into physical, mental, and artistic development.

The single primary vehicle for all learning, the factor that predicates everything, is interacting by communicating. Academics, special interests, and personal agenda are all secondary to the fact of people living together. That above all is the guiding reality. And it is the quality of that reality that is the focus and purpose of teaching by Archie and the faculty.

The setting is as unorthodox as the philosophy is exceptional. The students and faculty have constructed the school buildings and dormitory houses themselves, situated on an expanse of forested acreage surrounding a freshwater lake. Nearby is a small rural town. The responsibilities for the operation of the facility are collectively shared, which actually provide the context for a living curriculum, from gardening and animal husbandry, cleaning and laundry and doing dishes, repairs and maintenance, to ordering food and supplies, to planning, preparing, and serving meals.

The faculty is comprised of highly committed and distinctive individuals who seem fully aware of their role and impact as models. They are teachers, but even more, they are resources, catalysts, facilitators for actualizing each student's desires and interests, for inspiring their potential.

The effect is immediately evident. Never before have I met as many young children and adolescents who are so in touch with themselves, so at ease. They are direct, face-to-face, without the screen of self-effacement and affected shyness or brashness typical of youth.

The atmosphere is powerfully alive, full of sentience and seriousness and intelligence, of passion and fun and playfulness. It is a refuge, a sanctuary, as island of supportiveness and compassion and contemplation—yet equally a veritable hot-seat of confrontation and challenge and self-examination and accountability. Conflict is regarded as inevitable but as something to be resolved, not ignored or avoided. Solutions are not arbitrarily decided nor authoritatively imposed. And throughout the process of dealing with conflicts the aura of mutual respect is pervasive, which is, of course, an essential condition for learning self-respect.

A year ago I would not have even thought of it. Now, as I talk with Archie, it may be the perfect place for Sean.

Things move fast. I have had virtually no contact with Joan and Jeff since the failed affair with Mary and Stuart. When I informed them of the bizarre outcome they received it with no detectable emotion. If anything, it was as if they expected something of the sort, something to maintain their life of burden. Now when I tell them of Archie's school they seem indifferent, even detached, but are otherwise quick to give permission for Sean and I to visit overnight at the school.

With his usual placidness, Sean listens as I explain my plan.

What do you think?

He solemnly nods his head, looking at me. I do not take this apparent agreement without question, but I equally do not dismiss the possibility.

Our drive to the school is buoyant, a wondrous spring day, and we pass groves of orange trees that burst with white blossoms against the deeply green foliage, filling the air with a delicious, intoxicating fragrance. Sean is alert and companionable. I marvel at how companionable he is, this boy who does not communicate in any conventional way yet conveys his presence with such gentle clarity.

We are received with an easy warmth, and I sense everyone has already been informed of our coming and the nature of our stay.

It has been about two years since I last saw Archie, and we embrace. He greets Sean with a handshake. A couple of students introduce themselves and ask Sean if he would like to see the school. He looks at me. I say, if you want, sure, go ahead. And off they are, taking Sean by the hand along a path through the pine woods.

Archie and I catch up on each other's lives, and I meet the rest of the faculty. Eventually we join Sean at the lake where several of the students and faculty are enjoying the cool water.

Of course, Sean is ecstatic, with an occasional frenzy of flapping and blowing but staying with the others as part of them. The younger kids have taken well to him and include him in their play, splashing and diving and flipping him in and out of inflated inner tubes. Sean, playing with kids. Something not particularly special, something even innocuous, yet something Sean has never had an opportunity to do. His eyes sparkle with animation, his ripples of laughter mingling with the others.

That evening at supper Sean fills his plate and sits at a table with several children. He had already signed to me that he wanted to eat. He is made part of the cleanup crew and rinses dishes with another young boy. Sean rinses with zeal, taking a bit longer than necessary with all that running water, but he stays pretty focused with some reminders from the others in the crew.

Later, Archie tells Sean that he can sleep in a bunk with the young students or he can stay with me. He doesn't exactly choose but does not oppose when the kids enthusiastically invite him to go with them.

Overnight Sean had urinated in his bed and is helped in cleaning the sheets and blankets before he eats breakfast. Other than that possible anxiousness, Sean shows an ease of being here. I sense he is amazed at the relative freedom, always used to being confined to a room or house, always used to being under some form of scrutiny. Here, even though everyone is acutely aware of him and where he is, there is a sense of space, with a fundamental respect of personal borders. Perhaps he finds this somewhat familiar, as an echo of what I insistently established in our time together.

The bell is rung, indicating a group meeting of all residents. Everyone gathers in the large community building that serves as the meeting hall as well as kitchen, dining area, classroom, library, administrative office, and general social space.

The mood is one of respectful, alert silence as Archie begins by explaining the purpose of their coming together. Which of course everyone knows. But his acknowledging publicly that Sean is here to consider living with them grants a formality and a seriousness to something that affects them collectively. This is the opportunity for the issue to be fully, squarely critiqued, for doubts, concerns, questions, and opinions to be aired.

Sean is addressed personally and not abstractly talked about. He is not patronized. There is no doubt that he fully comprehends what is taking place and what is being said.

Each of the faculty speaks in turn, expressing his or her point of view regarding Sean. Some students make statements or ask questions. The emerging consensus becomes clear that Sean is welcomed. There is also an immediate understanding of the nature and magnitude of the responsibility involved both collectively and individually. Through discussion some of these responsibilities are determined, selecting Sean's dormitory mates, his kitchen partner, the primary faculty sponsor.

Throughout the meeting I absorb the sheer fact of what is unfolding here, these forty or so people spanning the ages from childhood to adult, assuming the concern for the reality of the life of this boy whom they have just met. Just as they assume the concern for every life in this room. The strength of their unity here is moving, an underlying bond that emanates a sense of belief in what they are doing. What they are doing is a very human thing, it is the essence of humanness. And humanness is the very thing that is so fragmented in Sean's life.

Throughout the meeting I watch Sean and see how surely he brings himself to his encounter, of forty people gathered for the express purpose of deciding whether they will invite him to live with them, forty people focused singularly upon him. And a year ago he could barely stand the encounter of just one person. The collective energy in the room is as remarkably warm and supportive as it is sobering and intense. Virtually everyone has spoken their agreement, voiced their acceptance. Now they want to know what Sean's choice is. It is his turn.

Esther looks at him and says in her gentle, confident voice, "Sean, we would like you to live with us if you want. If you don't that is perfectly okay. Let us know what you want to do."

Sean is looking at Esther, with the gaze of the room full of people quietly resting on him. Slowly, Sean nods his head.

As the gathering breaks up several of the students approach Sean, some shake his hand but many give him an eager spontaneous hug. Sean takes it all in, seeming a bit bewildered.

Before we leave the school that afternoon I take Sean to the lake. A few other people show up. It is quiet, soothing, a balance to the concentrated energy of the meeting.

I have Sean sit in a large inner tube with me and we paddle leisurely out to the floating platform. I tell him I like this place and these people very much, and I think it would be good for him to be here. I say it looks that you like it here too. I explain I will talk to his father and mother to arrange for it to happen, but it is their decision if he will come, not mine, not Archie's, not anyone at the school.

Steve has floated over in an inner tube with James, a boy of about eleven. Steve has elected to be Sean's faculty sponsor, assuming primary responsibility should he come.

Sean and I get back in our tube and soon we are in a water war with Steve and James, parrying and attacking and retreating. Having the obvious advantage of experience they flip us out of our tube first. Sean comes up from the water wide-eyed but grinning. After several bouts and many close calls, he and I finally manage to flip them.

The excitement becomes contagious. Students have maneuvered the huge truck inner tube from shore and evolve a

king-of-the-tube game. Smaller satellite tubes circle nearby.
Everyone is diving off and climbing into and falling from and
flipping out of inner tubes. The other students draw Sean into the
frolic, and while he does not exactly play with assertiveness, he
stays willingly involved. Even seems to enjoy it.
Steve and I drift off to the side of the activity and talk,
discussing tentative plans. He is very taken with Sean. He will
visit us in a few days, both to see Sean in another setting and to
keep some continuity alive. I am so encouraged by what is
unfolding here. As Sean and I leave I express my gratitude to
Archie, Steve, Esther, to the rest of the faculty and the students,
gratitude for this remarkable commitment to life they are carrying
out in the quiet forest.

Steve does come and stays for several days. He spends time
in the room, interested in what I do with the other boys and
getting more perspective on Sean. They do things together and
soon develop a rapport that is easy and apparent.
It is strange how I come to talk with Sean's parents about
the school's invitation. They avoid my attempts to meet with them
together, so I phone Jeff at his office, Joan at home. Once again,
Joan balks at "giving Sean up." The conditions are clear that any
visits would be greatly restricted and determined by the school
faculty. After many telephone calls they agree to visit the facility
one Saturday.
The following Monday, when I phone Joan, she says they
have decided that Sean will live at the school.

The next weekend, Jeff and Joan drive Sean there to stay.
I meet them, planning to be there three or four days to help Sean
adjust and to smooth the transition. They are nervous and awkward
as Sean's things are unloaded. Two suitcases. And a favorite
stuffed animal.
Sean's parents shift their feet and stall at the final moment,
the moment they have wished for and argued about and agonized
over countless times, no longer able to remain ambivalent. For the
moment is finally, unavoidably here. It is difficult for Joan to
control her emotion as she leans to kiss Sean on his cheek, holding

his shoulders with her hands. He stands woodenly. Jeff's eyes dart about like a wary animal's; he is clearly feeling out of his element. He thanks Archie and Esther and Steve, tells Joan it is time to go, and says goodbye to his son without ever touching him. Sadly, it seems more honest that way.

The bleakness of the departure passes quickly and Sean is soon absorbed into the vibrant life of the school over the next few days. He is greeted everywhere and responds with his breathy "Hhuhn." There always seems to be some student showing him a particular routine, a buddy to take him to play or walk through the woods. He is either involved in something or available to be involved. He may sit in the large community room leafing through a magazine while checking out all the activity that channels through there. Sometimes at night he is invited along into the television room with several kids. Some try to teach him ping-pong. He might hang around a dorm house while they tell stories. And he begins classes with Steve.

The social element is primary here, so unlike his life, where the social element has been deficient within his weirdness, his insulation, his removal. And he takes to it. It is as if he is—finally—ready for it.

The night before I am to leave several of us are sitting around in the comfortable home of Frank and Esther. Sean is sharing the large sofa with Esther, leaning casually against her. We talk about the options available for giving Sean as many opportunities as possible. They want to make clear to Sean what they expect of him and what in turn he can expect from them.

One thing they say—and they say to Sean—is they will expect him to communicate, somehow, for it is only fair that he let them know what he chooses and wants. No one wants to take over for him. They discuss having him visit the local elementary school where they know the teachers. Above all, they let Sean know they want him to be there. But never will he be forced.

Esther does most of the talking or monitors the questions and discussion. Her role is that of benevolent matriarch, preeminent authority grounded in unconditional love. Sean is readily drawn to her, not in any puppy-like dependency but more as if gathering nourishment and strength, the stirrings of autonomy.

Naturalness and vitality and supportiveness pervade the room, like a reassuring and exhilarating tonic. Sean already appears to be growing in solidity.

I no longer have to fear giving Sean up. I can give him over to these people whose collective energy and compassion will take up where I leave off. Where I must leave off.

This night, braced by the tonic in Frank and Esther's hand-built house, I feel immense gratitude, and I thank them all.

The next morning Sean and I go to the lake for an early swim. Our mood echoes the quiet stillness, the clarity of awakening, and we wade into the cool water. We are alone. I have told Sean the night before of my leaving and now have no reason or desire to break the sharing of silence with talk. Sean is calmly alert to the fullness of the moment. I sense that he has waves of thought and emotion, just as I do, about what his being here will bring, about our parting. He looks at me, at the mirrored surface of the water, at the surrounding trees, thinking to himself and passing feelings to me in his gaze.

After a time we both get out of the water together. We stand on the bank of pure white sand letting the sun warm and dry our nakedness. The air is sensual on glistening skin. We towel and dress. On the path to my car I have my arm around Sean's shoulders as he holds my waist. I kneel and he returns my hug with a direct even attention. It is at once an exchange of agreement, an understanding, one of sadness yet of strength and sureness.

He stands quietly, solidly, motionless while I get into my car, his eyes bright, accepting, expressive.

During the drive back my own thoughts and emotions race through me, washed along with splashes of sunlight and colors and fragrances and breezes. I alternate absorbing sensations of the passing landscape with the image of Sean's face and the range of feelings his memory evokes. I drive to the ocean and sit alone on the beach for several hours.

20

Moving On

"How have you worked this miracle?"
"By patience and by love, very simply. From their birth, I caress,
I solicit, I gently and pityingly insist."

Nikos Kazantzakis

The continuous rolling and swelling and breaking of the waves is
hypnotic and tranquilizing under the sky's blueness and the
caressing of the wind.
　　It is done.
　　I have seen it through to the miraculous.
　　I know Sean is now on the other side of his private hidden
tragedy. I am humbled and elated. Sean is a child who has ultimate
command in what he gives, and now he has opened to being part
of the world of people. I have stayed with Sean's outer life and I
have glimpsed his inner life with enough of both of know the
magnitude of risk he takes.
　　Risk, and I also see, trust.
　　Until now, steadfastly and masterfully he has refused this
world of ours, this world where we learn to exchange ourselves so
commonly and casually that we ignore the risk our lives bring
when trust and comfort and happiness and love cut both ways,
with pain and betrayal and ambiguity and rejection. Sean saw that
edge more keenly than most of us. He lived with it, razor sharp.

　　We are surrounded by dramas, take part in them, grow
accustomed to them. But what is not common is to intrude upon

them, enter them. That is not in the script, the singular drama of entering the lives of a family, insinuating ourselves into their particular inertia of stasis, their precarious tensions of power, of wrestling with the tortuous obscured dynamics.

I have changed the life of a child.

I have changed the life of this child, altered the course it would otherwise have taken without my entering.

There is life that is lived as an apparently seamless continuity of events, as a story line, however characterized with specialness and difficulties and mediocrities, which is the life that we typically believe and expect and therefore perpetrate.

Then there is life that is marked forever by seemingly random or accidental circumstance, a point in time that irrevocably changes the nature and direction a life takes.

I was not part of the seamless continuity of this family's story line. Our paths crossed. Sean's life and the lives of Joan and Jeff are marked forever, and the course their lives take is irrevocably altered.

I certainly have more than enough to keep me occupied by staying with the demands of the boys, of Nick and Philip and Lou and Billy. But even though their life circumstances are twisted and their particular strangenesses command the utmost vigilance, they do not reach me in the way Sean has, do not disturb me, haunt me with the same sheer poignancy of his life.

For no matter how aberrant and intense and imbalanced these boys may be the single essential difference between them and Sean is that they are not alone. Not in the way he has been, a barren, insular, hollow aloneness. That no matter how convoluted and dysynchronous are the dynamics of these boys and their families, there is still a bond, a continuity that ties them together. With them, I know I can work with the bond itself. Joan and Jeff had effectively kept Sean in such an emotional and psychological vacuum that whatever bond was ever there had long ago atrophied.

So although I am busy with these boys, the presence of Sean hovers with me, a glowing connection. For the first time in two years I can feel good about him, about his chances for some degree of a happy life. I realize I am connected to him in a special way and that this connection glows. I miss him, miss him in the way parents miss their child who has grown beyond them and into the first faltering steps of his own life.

I even find myself lightly tapping the wall with the backs of my fingers as I walk, or absently admiring the sheen of water on the surface of a table. Sean.

I talk regularly with Steve and Esther and Archie. I am not at all surprised at how quickly Sean has adapted to being there. More and more he is involving himself, if not always by active participation and initiation, then by his attentive presence.

I had wanted to step beyond the tenuousness of going one-on-one with Sean, an arrangement that is so ripe for the sabotage and testing of wills that became so familiar. With the sheer number and variety of personalities and styles at the school, Sean is entreated and even compelled into their society, bypassing the potential skewing of exclusive encounters. Sean clearly prefers people. And it is not the anonymity of the herd, where he can slip into the crowd unnoticed. There is a constant flow of interaction, acknowledgement, engagement. He is noticed. Moreover, he is demanded upon, but within a context of support and encouragement better suited to avoiding the dogfights of trying to go head-to-head.

Demonstrably, Sean wants to be there. Three days after his arrival he walked out and was found on the road toward town, miles from the school. A collective meeting was held and again all the residents declared their desire and welcome for Sean, yet his staying was entirely his own choice. If he wanted to leave they would certainly help him do so. He was asked if he wanted to return to his parents. Slowly, he turned his head from side to side. No.

Sean had shown he knew how to leave. He never did it again.

He rotates with the various kitchen duties, washes his own clothes and linens in the laundry, prepares his own meals and snacks and cleans up. He is a quick learner.

He takes the public bus every day into town for class in the local school. He still uses the same basic signs from our time together but is also voicing several simple words and word approximations. Hi and bye or goodbye, some of the faculty and student names, some foods and objects.

I call the school and sometimes Sean is given the phone. It is strange to hear him say "Hi," to attempt my name with a drawn "Daae." I talk to him a little and then we exchange goodbyes. His voice is still a bit rough and plosive but at the same time more even and calm than before, as if he really is trying to communicate and not just imitate or react. As I talk I also have the strong sense of Sean truly listening to me, and although he is not speaking in return and there is not conversation in any usual way, I feel we connect nonetheless.

Jeff and Joan were given a discounted tuition but are delinquent in their payments. Archie tells me that the school will absorb any loss rather than have Sean leave. Their commitment is solid.

Sean goes with his parents for Christmas. They drive to pick him up and return him in two days. Esther tells me their awkwardness was sad to witness and doubts they will want any more visits. Soon after, I learn that Joan and Jeff have moved to another city much further away, a new life for them, and they leave Sean in the care of the school.

I drive to visit Sean for what turns out to be the last time.

He greets me with a clear "Hi" and a good try at my name. We embrace and I realize how much he has grown, filled out, matured both physically and in the way he carries himself. He seems glad to see me and is in a good-natured, spirited mood. I say I am happy to see him and that he looks great.

I ask him to show me his room and he leads me to his dorm house which he shares with three other students. His area is boyishly arranged, disarrayed but basically tidy. I notice his stuffed animal. It has been a hot, sticky day so I say let's swim. We change our clothes and I see the slightly thicker muscles of his long limbs, the tentative sproutings of genital hair. The timing was critical. How significantly different his puberty would be if he still were with Joan and Jeff.

We walk through the paths leading to the lake and I ask how he likes being here. He doesn't respond, so I say his name, asking him again. He looks at me, then nods his head. Students greet us as we near the lake. Sean responds with his own "Hi." The water feels deliciously clean and cooling. We stay in the shallows, just leisurely bobbing and taking short underwater swims. Sean and I share a warm easy familiarity, but there is also something else, something new between us. It is the difference of our lives, of our individual lives, that we are no longer of the same world, the same intensely focused arena. Sean is on his own path now and no longer in that arena; no longer do I need to confront him there. It is a mutual, silent understanding. He now has some ownership, he is empowered. I am no longer part of his life, not here. If anything, I am part of him in memory and perhaps affection.

There is no need to talk. We squat on the white sand bank. Sean lightly taps the sheen of water at his feet with casual elegance, looks at me. I somewhat reflexively imitate his gesture, sighing, and gaze around at the trees, the sky. Sean rises and comes to me, fixing me with his penetrating eyes. He reaches and touches my cheek with the back of his hand, holding it there for in indeterminate moment, still looking into my eyes, speaking nothing, saying everything.

He drops his hand to take mine, and we walk back to the community building in time for supper.

Epilog

His was a full reality, one of a number of equally valid truths.

Joanne Greenburg

I stayed with Sean's life for over two years.

Then I stopped.

I have not returned to see him again. And I have not returned to be with other children of such staggering intensity again.

The parallel will not let go of me.

Sean lived a strange balance of being virtually alone with his difference while the world he knew adjusted to him. Sean was insistently expected to change, to somehow become more normal, but without any real pathways. He could not do it alone. He was left alone and by that distance commanded a certain power within his surrounding life. Yet the final irony, the real tragedy, is that he was powerless in the process of determining the outcome of his being different.

I crossed the invisible, undefined threshold of his aloneness as well as what kept him alone, upset that balance by intruding into those worlds, collapsing the distance. I was expected to make Sean more normal. I could not do it alone.

Like Sean, I too was disturbing to those around me in my efforts and attempts, in the very fact of my intrusions. I too was left alone within this strange arena, balanced by the immediate life around me that adjusted to me, accommodated me, but did not understand, encourage, nor support what I was doing. I had a certain power within the world of this child and his family—an astonishing, serious power, a power that changed lives—but returning across the threshold, I was essentially without significance to alter the outcome of his perceived difference. It was more fortuitous than by any design that I made the connection with Archie and his school. And that it worked.

Just who Sean was became in effect a statement about who was defining him. Sean was as much a composite of consensus agreement from the world around him—from those who knew him least, who balked at confronting, entering, and somehow understanding his reality—as he was singularly, maddingly, difficult to reach and to know.

I saw Sean through a different set of lenses, without any consensus, and found him to be other than he was presumed to be. I wrenched my life apart in order to reach and address this child, this person, and after two years I stopped because I could no longer do it alone.

The parallel holds.

What I learned with Sean echoes through every disturbing child I have ever known, through everything I have ever done with them. It echoes everywhere, through being with other children, through what is done with children, echoes through what we do with one another. It continues echoing through my life.

Still, from time to time, I find that I tap things, in a light quick rhythm, with the backs of my fingers.

Postscript

When I decided to write about Sean I did so from several viewpoints. My educational and professional training had provided me with extensive armaments of theories, strategies, and techniques, but nothing truly sufficient to prepare me for the impact of encountering a deeply aberrant child. Throughout my career I came to learn from my own experience and equally through observation of other professionals given charge of these children's lives, virtual wholesale charge, that treatment was based on the assumption of the child as victim. The child was presumably in the grip of some horrid, inaccessible malaise that above all—most frighteningly—obviated any sense of self. The child was to have no ability or experience of autonomy, no central "I," no control, even no volition. Treatment spoke the language of medicine and rehabilitation. Cure, training.

For parents and families this belief was a worthy straw to grasp, treading water as they often were in the awful reality of the child's remote and bizarre strangeness. They, in fact, had felt themselves victim enough. They had to live with it, the almost alien presence of this child, unrecognizable as issuing from their own lives.

But what I was seeing was an expropriation of the very thing necessary to break the frozen inertia of unconnectedness. What was being expropriated was the recognition in the child of an autonomous, central, volitional self.

The specialists with their jargon and diagnoses, the programs with their patronizing methodologies, the schools with their simian-like compliance training, the families with their desperate fear and guilt all missed the point.

The child is not vacant, not absent, not out of touch. The child is acutely—if painfully—unwaveringly—if idiosyncratically—present. The child does not need the significant persons of the world around him to base their interactions on the belief that no one is home. The child may well be disturbing, may well be confused, may well be tragically hurt, may well be incapable of going it alone, but what is most needed is a mutual recognition of self. The child must see, or sense, or feel a reflection of his own human self in that of another.

I saw that people were so distraught because of this child they backed away, consistently, almost reflexively. It was rejection, but more than that, it was distaste, disgust, disdain. It was dismissal of the child as person. And I wondered for the child how much of that anyone could be expected to take.

Our social practices too often treat people with little or no respect, where individuals are not that important. Children are treated even less so, indulged perhaps, patronized regularly, tolerated generally, but their individual uniqueness and significance is supplanted by grooming them for their larger mission in life, as members, workers, consumers in the social matrix.

But a curious phenomenon has been occurring with increasing frequency. Educationally, less and less children are fitting this normative training. More and more of them are not adjusting, showing up with problems that are met with specialized teaching, counseling, remediation, or treatment. Are we as a society only now truly recognizing the thousands of these problem children that have previously gone undetected? No, I think not. I think instead we are seeing a serious systemic deficiency, the inability of our social structures to adapt to the individual differences of children and so, in turn, attempting to force them into narrower and narrower holes.

I see how children are constantly shuffled around, lectured to, solicited, assigned, directed, coerced, threatened, bribed, punished. Then, a certain predictable proportion of them will be diagnosed, categorized, labeled, medicated, experimented with, warehoused. What seems common to all is the impersonal, indifferent image of the institutions and the attitude of the people who work in them, institutions ostensibly designed and people specifically trained to understand children. There is no embracing atmosphere of humanness, of caring, of affection, of enjoyment.

Under the guise of educational and professional expertise, children are shuffled around and their personalities shaped and their self-esteem arbitrated—and, in fact, the outcome of their lives determined—by a constant stream of professional strangers. Ultimately, scores of children are left alone with their peculiar and necessary devices of adaptation and survival.

Sean is an extreme example of a person lost in this complex web of perceptions and assumptions, and as well a symptom of the familial and social inability to address its individuals.

Which brings me to what is probably the most important purpose of writing about him. I wanted to illustrate the nature of being with this boy, a child of difficulty, but a child nonetheless. I wanted to convey and describe my attempts to formulate a path to approach him, attempts that were severe at times, risky at others, always demanding, but also within the scope of possibility.

I deliberately avoided defining myself or specifically my role with Sean. I intentionally wanted to present this as a personal process more than a professional one, to emphasize that here is a human condition in many ways common to us all. I wanted a reader to identify something to be able to project onto, not restricted or prevented by any perceived lack of training or expertise. I wanted my experiences to be accessible. And I wanted to show this as pertaining to anyone who encounters children, particularly for families who may be pulled by the myriad explanations and prescriptions given for dealing with their own.

If nothing else, I wanted to provoke.

This most dark area of aberrant children is itself left uncritiqued, unchallenged, unexplored. It concerns all children as it concerns all of society. I wanted to provoke a reader into questioning not only what my experiences were with Sean, but to consider how and why he developed that way. Into reviewing assumptions of child rearing and development, of how children are viewed and treated. And left alone.

I wanted to provoke more than I presumed to provide answers for. In many respects I purposely left a great deal unsaid, at the risk of some ambiguity, than I wanted to present a completed story, neatly packaged. I wanted to prevent leaving the impression that Sean should be understood—intellectually, academically, scientifically, professionally—as fundamentally or categorically different from anyone else, in a manner that would view him independently of the context of his life.

I wanted to prevent the conclusion that a disturbance such as Sean presented can be sufficiently explained, and explained away.

I believe instead that the reality of these phenomena is not in our descriptions; that the descriptive process is the very thing that distances the child and alienates others from him. The reality lies rather in our experiences with the child, in what we do, as a parent, as a relative, as a professional, as an institution, as a society.

My experience with Sean is a constellation of my work with many children and families that evolved over several years. An evolution that was itself a series of trials and errors, an elusive choreography of theory, intuition, methodology, strategy.

This is but a single story out of the many others I could, and perhaps one day will, write. To regard any of these encounters as successes—or failures—is difficult for me, in fact unsettling, and may be the underlying reason why I have backed away from such intense work.

Because invariably I did reach each child. I feel I was able to break through a child's devices and validate a quivering, unrealized self.

But I came to realize the larger picture, the ongoing context of that child's life, which did not provide the vital and necessary support to bridge what I had only began. Remember, a child is powerless, but these children were so immersed in powerlessness that in the eyes of parents and schools and clinicians not only was the child's fledgling identity not taken seriously—not even recognized—so neither was my advocacy of it.

I shocked them all. I said, "Look, this is a person." They didn't want to hear it. I cannot stress enough: these children are to be left alone. We don't want to know their stories. Over and over again I reached a child, knowing it could be done, bypassing the myths and pronouncements, the fear and guilt. I did it as a model—not an expert, not a magician—to show a way for parents and teachers and specialists to collectively, supportively carry it on. So, although I may have succeeded in touching the dormancy and bewilderment of the child's self, and in most cases catalyzing it into newly expressed form and display, alone I could not supply sufficient continuity and substance and variety for this self to truly grow. This is an aggregate human concern and responsibility, the necessary context for any person's life.

Sadly, too often it just wasn't there. Parents split up. Families divided. Specialists argued. Teachers balked. Administrators resisted.

I found that I solicited the child, deeply, sincerely, with my entire being. Come on, open up, trust, it's worth it. And I did this without the deceptive fostering of dependency but rather of instilling a self-reliance, and when he did come out, thrashing and joyous and awkward and painful and embarrassing, the world I entreated him to open to still backed away.

But I have no regrets. I rest in the belief that I gave each of these children something, something unassailable in the face of their dehumanized, custodial lives. It may not ever be recognized, or acknowledged, but remain simply a private, internal knowing. For the child, for myself.

Although I have continued to involve my career with children, I do not work with those so unsettling, so disturbing. I do not go to see Sean or any of the others, and have not for many years. When I did, having been out of their lives in any real way, I felt I only reminded them—and me—of our mutual helplessness. Ours eyes would lock momentarily and the gates would open, our hearts flooded. Too much, just too much.

Further Readings

Greenfeld, Josh. *A Child Called Noah: A Family Journey.* Harcourt, Brace, Jovanovich, 1989.

Heller, Joseph. *Something Happened.* Dell, 1989.

Hulme, Keri. *The Bone People: A Masterful Story of Myth and Emotional Healing.* Viking Penguin, 1986.

Kaufman, Barry N. *Son-Rise.* Warner Books, 1984.

Laing, R.D. *The Facts of Life.* Pantheon, 1984.

Lovaas, O. Ivar. *The Autistic Child: Language Development Through Behavior Modification.* Irvington, 1986.

Pearce, Joseph Chilton. *The Magical Child.* Bantam, 1981.

Rothenberg, Mira. *Children with Emerald Eyes.* NAL-Dutton, 1987.

Index

About the Author

DAVID C. CIPOLLONI is a Child Specialist who has worked in Florida hospitals, its university system, and public schools. He now consults independently to child care agencies and preschool programs. This is his first book.